Sharing the Journey

Sharing the Journey

❖

a psychotherapist reflects on her work

Judith A. Goren, PhD

iUniverse, Inc.
New York Lincoln Shanghai

Sharing the Journey
a psychotherapist reflects on her work

iUniverse, Inc.

For information address:
iUniverse, Inc.
2021 Pine Lake Road, Suite 100
Lincoln, NE 68512
www.iuniverse.com

"Bag of Tricks" first appeared in *The AHP Perspective*, newsletter of the Association for Humanistic Psychology (July/August, 1996).
"Remembering" was given an award in the annual spring reading series (1998) sponsored by Detroit Women Writers.

ISBN: 0-595-32494-0

Printed in the United States of America

To my husband, Bob,

whose love has made everything else possible

Contents

Part IV   Pitfalls, Problems and Puzzles

Part V   Saying Goodbye

Acknowledgements

I want to give thanks to many good friends and family members who read and critiqued drafts of this work in various stages: my psychologist colleagues: Gayle Beck, Sara Byer, Katherine Young and Sid Berkowitz; co-members of our poetry workshop: Mitzi Alvin, Lorene Erickson, Patricia Hooper and Elizabeth Anne Socolow; other writer-friends: Kitty Dubin, Larry Dubin, Manny Frisch and Robert Rosenzweig. I also want to thank my son, Steve Goren, for his invaluable suggestions about organization and titles, as well as his general editing capabilities and my husband, Bob Goren, who read every chapter as soon as it was completed and in its many subsequent revisions. Special thanks also to Judith Guest, who sent me pages of typed notes filled with her great enthusiasm and excellent suggestions, and to Dan Minock, who provided essential editorial feedback on the entire final version as well as an earlier one. Thanks also to my dear friend Julia Press, who has provided encouragement and support throughout this project, and to my grandson, Rob Goren, who has been my computer consultant for all technical aspects of manuscript preparation.

Prologue:
Paradoxes of Psychotherapy

Psychotherapy is a form of work that has many paradoxes. As I have moved further away in time from that profession which occupied me so completely for so many years, the contradictions have become more sharply defined for me.

As anyone who has participated in a psychotherapy session or seen one depicted on film knows, the basic structure looks like this: the therapist sits in one chair, the client sits in another, and they talk.

It sounds simple, but it is very complex: that is the first paradox. The depth and change-oriented nature of the talk, the informed nature of the listening, and the purposeful responses of the therapist, distinguish this interchange from ordinary conversation.

These two human beings are engaged in what may be one of the most basic functions of talking since the human race developed speech: one person telling his troubles to another. Yet psychotherapy is distinctly a phenomenon that began in the latter half of the 20th century, and largely in the western countries. So a second paradox is that it is both age-old and yet a modern, culture-bound phenomenon.

Psychotherapy, like sex, is an anomaly: millions of people engage in it, yet it is so intimate and private that no one knows for sure what really goes on behind someone's closed door.

Psychotherapy can involve communication at the deepest level of human intimacy. But, another contradiction: the intimacy is one-way. The client reveals all to the therapist, but the therapist does not respond in kind. If she did, the work would risk becoming non-therapeutic.

Work: that is yet another irony. This interchange is both spiritual and commercial. The very soul of the client is being exposed, touched, healed. The most vulnerable, painful areas of one's life are entered and reentered. The client enters a dark labyrinth, and the therapist is there at every step, holding up a light. But the work ends after 50 minutes and a check is written, or an insurance company is billed.

Insurance provides another set of contradictions. Limits on the number of visits, monitoring of the reasons the client is there at all, evaluation of what progress he is making, permission to continue for a few more weeks a relationship that needs to go on for a few more years, interference by a stranger in this most delicate and intimate work: the balance between privacy and managed care approval is a new and most distressing phenomenon in our list of paradoxes. Certainly, without the HMO, many people who would never be able to afford even one session can now be helped. But, once having stepped into the sacred arena, they are often thrown out against their will and against the best professional judgment of the psychotherapist. For the therapist, there is the problem of balancing the privacy of the client against the need for information on the part of the supplier.

Psychotherapy is both a science and an art. Psychiatry, which is a branch of the medical profession, and Clinical Psychology, which is a specialization in the broader field of Psychology, have classified human beings and their behaviors and emotional quirks into many neatly labeled boxes containing diagnostic categories, social profiles, neuroses, psychoses, and personality disorders of all types. In addition, there are dozens of therapeutic schools, approaches, methodologies, theories, practices and interventions designed to help the suffering human beings in the above boxes and categories to change their lives. The paradox is: when two people are alone in the therapy room, the effectiveness of the therapist is an art. A well-trained professional must be grounded in the scientific knowledge of the field. Advanced degrees and professional credentials are most useful. But, essentially, what the therapist says or does in that private room with that client is based on the right balance between good sense, intuition, and the life experience of the therapist herself. Both science and art are necessary components of effective psychotherapy.

Connected to the above is the paradox of structure vs. non-structure in the work. Therapy works best, I learned early in my training, if the client and the therapist agree on a goal, and work toward it. The best way to get to your destination, if you are on a driving trip, is to know where you want to go and have a road map that helps you get there. I began that way with each client. "Why are you here? Where would you like to be? How can I help you get there?" I learned to ask these questions in a way less blunt than they may sound on paper. I learned that only the first question, "Why are you here?" is easy for clients to answer. *I'm depressed. I'm anxious all the time. I can't sleep. My boyfriend just broke up with me. My boss hates me. I hate my job. I can't get along with my mother/father/coworkers/ husband. The kids are driving me crazy. I'm 46 and I don't know what I want to do when I grow up. I have nightmares and feel scared. I can't decide whether to break up with my boy/girlfriend or get married.*

The answers to the other questions evolve over time. They may seem clear to the therapist, but often the client is so distressed that she/he cannot envision life to be any different than it is and has been. To reach even this first step, the process of envisioning something different and better, may take several sessions.

The paradox is that to work within a goal-oriented structure, it is, nonetheless, sometimes most effective to let individual sessions flow with freedom. To reach the goal, it is often necessary to let the client wander a bit, to leave the main highway and explore some tree-lined country roads. In those moments, the client may reveal the true issue or problem, of which he was not even aware until his words led to a memory or a buried emotion that now wells up in a way that is undeniable to him. This process opens inner doors and broadens his perception. Then, with expanded vision and understanding, he can look down from the hill where his wanderings have led him, and see clearly that the town he wanted to reach before dusk is right below him, its lights beginning to shine. He knows where he is headed.

It is very difficult to explain this to a managed care consultant who insists that you take the route along the freeway.

Another paradox is ease vs. fatigue. To all outer appearances, what I did all day was to sit in a comfortable chair in a pleasant room and listen to the stories of people whom, for the most part, I enjoyed being with, whom I liked. The paradox was that at the end of a full day, I often felt exhausted. In my earlier years, I could see eight or nine people in a day and not be too tired; by the final year of my work, I found that seeing five, even with an hour break for lunch, was the limit of my comfort zone. Four was even better.

At the times when I felt fatigue, it did not come from the nature of the information being imparted to me. Rather, it came from the degree of intensity and concentration I held. Sometimes it also came from battling, verbally or at a more silent level, the resistance or shut-down energy of some clients toward my interventions, interpretations, suggestions or questions.

So, after a day just sitting in a quiet room in a comfortable chair, "chatting," as one of my clients preferred to refer to our interactions, I only wanted to go home and curl up on the sofa and read the morning paper.

From the perspective of the therapist, another paradox is the way in which this work can be deeply troubling and yet so deeply satisfying. This statement could, of course, be made about any form of work. The difference here is that I am not talking about the nature of working conditions or anything external, but the way the work impacts the psyche of the therapist. One troubling aspect is how the issues of the client resonate with unresolved issues of the therapist. A depressed therapist has difficulty functioning after a day with depressed clients; a therapist's unresolved conflicts with her mother are mirrored when a client comes in with those very issues; a therapist who has dissociated her own memories of childhood abuse may find she is having nightmares after working with a client (or, these days, clients) who are recalling their own memories. For these reasons, of course, it is essential to good therapy that the therapist clear up her own issues before attempting to help someone else. Otherwise, her unconscious resistance may lead the client away from where he needs to take his own explorations.

However, even if the therapist has dealt, in her own therapy, with her past and present problems, there is another troubling aspect: at night, after the work of the sessions has been completed, there remain the images that paraded through her office all day. Images of a child being ignored, neglected, slapped, belt-whipped, raped. Images of a child waiting for a parent who never came, a promise never kept, a death never understood. The knowing that the child I see in my mind is the suffering adult who comes to my office each week. And it is not one child or adult; it is many, daily. The images flash in and out of my awareness. I can no longer watch the myriad of TV dramas based on true stories; they are banal compared to the inner pictures I have carried home from my office. I weep, not when I am with my clients, but when I read the newspaper each day, read the repetition of the same stories I have been hearing, still happening to other children a generation later. This is a wound the therapist must bear.

But there is the joy of the work. The indescribable satisfaction of being permitted to touch the soul of another human being, to see change, to watch a healing take place. The privilege of being invited into the secret, dark vault where another's hidden secrets reside. The excitement of sharing a discovery process, the equivalent of being a detective, an archaeologist and a jungle guide. The creative process of joining the imagery of the client to help his inner world open to him. The moment-to-moment feeling of rightness and relief when you help the client descend a dark staircase, or climb a sunlit mountain path; when each of you, metaphorically hand in hand, take a step and the next step appears, and after that the next, and you know when to proceed, or when to stop for the time being. You know what to say, or when to say nothing, to take the journey deeper, or to make it feel safer. All of it is a creative process. The satisfaction at the end of a really good session, for me, is the same as when I produce a new poem, or a painting, or a chapter in this book.

Paradox: there are sometimes sessions that flow beautifully, smoothly but, even over much time, the outer life of the client does not improve. Then, there are sessions where I think nothing at all happened, when I think afterward, *I am wasting my time doing this work,* but, for the client, the work was life altering, leading to changes and improvements I never would have expected. "It all was because you said…" someone tells me a few years later. And I don't even remember saying that. Perhaps I didn't; perhaps that is what they remembered, inaccurately, that I said. It doesn't matter: the client's life/attitude/mood/has improved. He accomplished that, not I. But I was there as a participant, or at least as a witness. There is still joy.

These, then, are some of the paradoxes of my profession: it is simple but complex, age-old but culture-bound, employs one-way intimacy, is both spiritual and commercial, private but public, both a science and an art, goal-oriented and free-flowing, physically easy but exhausting, troubling yet satisfying. The apparent success or failure of the session does not always correlate with the client's life changes.

This, undoubtedly, is not an exhaustive list. Even as I conclude this chapter, another possible paradox comes to mind: psychotherapy as we know it, a field which has grown rapidly to touch and change the lives of hundreds of thousands of people, could be on its way out. Will the combination of new medications for curbing psychoses and altering moods, along with the time restrictions of managed care and a new call for objective quantification of results, make this anomalous profession obsolete? And if that happens, will society be any the worse?

Only the coming decades hold the answer.

PART I

As Therapy Begins: Ground Rules and Self Care

Screening Phone Calls

It is a quarter to one. I am sitting at my desk eating a sandwich I prepared this morning, turkey with honey mustard dressing on fresh Jewish bakery rye bread. I have ten minutes before the next session begins. The phone rings.

I have a decision to make. If I answer it, my brief lunch time may be spent with someone who wants to change a scheduled time, meaning a juggling in my appointment book; with an insurance company phoning me back, in which case I do not want to miss the call; with a client who is feeling "down" and wants nurturing; with someone canceling an appointment, who will want to explain why in great detail.

Or, this could be a potential client, a call which takes time and alertness. I must make a quick decision. In the next few minutes, I want to make myself a cup of herbal tea in the microwave, visit the ladies room, repair my lipstick and stretch my muscles, which are stiff from a morning of sitting in one place. But I also want to make sure that if this is a new client, I do not miss out. I decide to let the answering machine take the call.

The caller does not leave a message. I am frustrated and wonder what opportunity I missed. Perhaps, I console myself, it was just another call for the furniture store whose number is one digit apart from mine.

The first call from a potential client is somewhat like the introduction to a blind date. Just as a woman learns when she is phoned for a blind date that it is not always wise to say "yes" too quickly, so I learned, after some mishaps, that it is wise to do some telephone interviewing. As with a blind date, I want to know who this person is and where he or she got my number. There are other questions: *What is the nature of the situation for which she is seeking help? Am I the right person to help with that kind of problem? Does he sound like someone I want to spend time with? Does he sound open to being helped? Can she afford my services?* The caller may have questions for me, as well. A prospective client may ask me "Are you experienced in dealing with (depression/divorce/alcohol treatment, etc.)?" Other equally important questions for the client to ask are, "What is your fee?" and "Will my insurance cover your services?"

All of these questions must be held in mind in the brief second between the therapist saying, "Hello?" and the person on the other end saying, "I want to make an appointment with you."

Experience has taught me that it is wiser, initially, to let the machine take the call, so that I can prepare myself for the conversation. I have learned to tell a great deal about the caller from his voice, his way of speaking and the content of the message. That is one reason I never used a secretarial service to answer my calls: I want to hear the message and the voice for myself.

Not picking up the phone immediately also gives me a chance to look at my appointment schedule to decide if I have time for a new client. I might have time this week, but only because two people are out of town. After that I could feel overloaded. Or, I might not have time this week, but a regular client with a standing appointment is in the process of ending her work with me, and will only be coming a few more times. Perhaps I can offer the new person that time slot.

I listen carefully as the message comes through on my tape. There are some calls I want to respond to at a later time. If the call is regarding an area of expertise that is not my preference, I can check with my colleagues for their availability and call back with helpful information. (I choose not to work with people who are psychotic or actively alcoholic, for example. I also choose to work only with adults or young adults, not with children or adolescents. These are choices I can make in private practice. A psychotherapist working for someone else may be assigned clients and not have these options.)

How can I tell on the phone if this is a person I want to spend time working with? It is a matter of intuition based on experience. If the caller tells me she has just fired her last three therapists, but her best friend told her how wonderful I was, I'm doubtful. My ego says, "I will be the one to succeed with her." But my wiser self replies, "If you take her on, there is a 95% chance that you, too, will end up fired." Whether I say *Yes* or *No* often depends on whether my caseload is up or down. Usually my wiser self is correct.

Whether or not the person's schedule fits with mine is always an issue. If someone works an hour's drive away and has only a 30 minute break for lunch, the appointment must be in the evening or on a Saturday. In the later years of my career, I chose to work no later than 6:00 p.m. I never worked on Saturday. If those facts were established first, the conversation need go no further. I would make a referral. Once, however, when I bent my own rule, I was glad. There was something about the woman on the other end of the phone that I liked immediately. I felt she would be a rewarding person for me to know and work with. She could, if she hurried, get to my office by 6:30. At first, after I agreed to do this, I had a brief pang of regret. What if I didn't like working with her as well as I believed? Did I want to extend my day that long, even if just one night a week? But my first intuition was correct: she was a caring, competent person in a difficult circumstance that was not of her doing, she was open and receptive to help, and made excellent progress. I looked forward to our sessions and was glad I had followed my instincts in that first call.

Some callers really don't want help. Once, a woman called to make an appointment. But for every opening I gave her, she had a reason why she couldn't take it. "I bowl on Mondays. No, I have a luncheon date on Tuesday." We went through my available hours. "I could come at 9:00 AM on Friday," she finally decided.

"I don't come in on Fridays" I told her. "And on the days I do come in, I begin at 10:00."

"Well," she said, "maybe you could come in just this Friday at 9:00 and we could meet and then I'll see. If my bridge group goes to Florida for the winter, then maybe I could come on Wednesdays at 9:00, before my beauty shop appointment."

We never did make an appointment. I was not sorry.

I have just finished my turkey sandwich when the phone rings again. Fate is giving me a second chance, but again I gamble, clearing my desk of crumbs, crusts and plastic wrap as I listen. This time a clear voice on the machine says, "My name is Mary Smith. You come highly recommended by my cousin. I am dealing with a series of recent losses, and would like to see you for therapy. I am laid off of my job, and can come any time. You can call me back any time this afternoon. My number is…" I take the call long enough to ask if I may phone her back at four o'clock, when I will be free to talk.

I phone back at ten of four and we make our first appointment. I look forward to meeting this woman. She sounds intelligent, her issues are within my range of expertise, our available times match, she has good insurance coverage, and, most important, I sense her sincerity and motivation. This, I sense, will be a successful blind date.

First Meeting

It is noon. I am expecting a new client. It is her first visit. Like the second stage of a blind date scenario, this may be a one-time event or it could lead to a long and complex relationship. All I know about her comes from a brief phone conversation a week earlier: her name, approximate age, marital status and the general nature of why she is coming to see me. I also have an impression of her from the tone and timbre of her voice and the way in which she expressed herself. I have thought about these meager clues during the past week, and have spent the past ten minutes focused on them, trying to intuit a sense of this person who will walk through my door at any moment. I feel a sense of anticipation as a new challenge is about to begin, and a little nervousness.

I review the kinds of questions I want to ask her, the information I feel will be useful for putting her life into a large context for my understanding, and for hers. Chiefly, of course, I want to know why she is here. But in addition, there is information I need to gather as we talk. This includes a general picture of her current lifestyle; her family-of-origin background; current health problems and previous therapy. Is she here to make plans for ongoing treatment, or is this just a one-time consultation?

If she plans to continue with me, I also want to save time during this session to clarify the business aspects of therapy: payments, insurance, broken appointments, phone calls between sessions, and to plan future time slots for her. If I believe we can work well together, I hope she will feel she has gained something from this first session and will plan to return. Also of importance, in case she wants to work with me but I do not believe we are a good match, I need to have some referral names ready, as well as a reason why I am referring her: not a rejection, but a better opportunity for her.

That is *my* agenda for the first session. It may have nothing to do with her agenda.

She is hurting. It took much inner debate and swallowing of pride to make the first phone call to me. She wants me to like her, to understand her, to help her, to solve her problem for her. She is hoping for some magic words to make her pain go away. She may want to tell me, at great length, how she is right and her husband/mother/co-worker is wrong. She may want to tell me something she has never told another living soul, and she is terrified to tell me because she doesn't even know me. She may have been suffering from anxiety or depression for a long time.

This is like a blind date for her, too.

She probably knows even less about me than I know about her. She may have received my name from a trusted friend or relative or from her doctor or lawyer. Or I may be more anonymous than that: she may have found me through a professional referral service or the yellow pages. She doesn't know if she will feel comfortable with me. She is thinking about how to present herself. She is nervous.

We are about to meet. She wants me to make the hurt go away; I need to gather and impart information. More than that, I need to establish a sense of rapport with her. Without that, she may not return, and the information will be of no use. How will we reconcile our two separate agendas?

I hear her come into the waiting room. (I know she is there because the door squeaks, my substitute for a receptionist.) I go out and introduce myself. Now, at last, we each see a real human being, face to face. I hand her a brief intake form to fill out, and tell her I will return for her in a few moments. In that contact, I gain a further impression: her degree of calmness or agitation, her ability to make contact with me, her degree of openness. There is a double purpose in this interaction: I need the basic information on the form (address, phone numbers, birth date, emergency contact person); for her, filling it out is a concrete task that, hopefully, helps her to focus and reduce some of her initial anxiety.

I leave her alone to fill out the form, then return and invite her into my office. I begin by asking if this is her first time seeing a therapist, which gives her a chance to express any ambivalence she may have about being in here. If it is not her first time, I ask about previous therapy. Sometimes I am surprised to find out that the client is still in therapy with someone else, but is having some difficulty and is "shopping around." If that is the case, I urge her to work things out first with the other therapist, telling her this will be just a consultation session and I will not see her again until after she has officially terminated with the other person.

If she is not in therapy now, but has been in the past, I generally want to know why she did not choose to return to the other therapist. It is important to the prognosis of future work to know whether she quit when the going got rough, or whether the person she was seeing moved to another city, leaving her with the issue of loss, or whether it was just so long ago that she forgot who the other therapist was.

This conversation is akin to the blind date in which the two people ask each other, "Have you ever been married? In a long-term relationship? What happened?" and so forth.

If the new client has never been in therapy, I may ask her what she was expecting. Sometimes I find out that she had envisioned me sitting behind a big desk or that she had feared I would ask her to lie down on a couch, as she has seen in the movies. Actually, we are in two armchairs, facing each other. If she seems nervous, I reassure her that we will just be talking, and that I want to find out why she is here and also to get some information from her.

Then she tells me why she came.

I have probably asked her that in the first phone call, and may refer back to what she told me then. On the phone, I would have said, "Would you sum up, in a few words, why you want to come in: is it a marital problem? Depression? Job difficulties?" This information gives me some focus, and lets me know if it is a situation I want to take on. Now, in my office, I may say, "You told me, in the phone call, that you're having problems with your boss and you feel anxious all the time. Can you tell me more about that?"

As she talks, I may interject clarifying questions about the symptoms she has labeled "anxiety," and about her situation with her boss. In that way, she can pour out her story, and I can find out much of the background I need to begin a working therapeutic relationship.

Another task I have in the 50 minutes of that first session is to give her some idea of what "therapy" is about: what we will do together in sessions, what I may ask of her between sessions, and what she can do immediately to reduce her anxiety level. It is important that she understand this is a team effort. While I may offer suggestions from time to time, the important part of the work comes from our joint identification of how she perpetuates her difficulties and how she might think and behave differently. She needs to know that she, ultimately, is the agent of her own change. My role is to guide her in making that happen. Thus, the real power belongs to her.

If we have made a good connection, and she is willing to make another appointment, often much of the anxiety she has carried in has dissipated by the end of the session.

If her problem is depression, I mentally assess whether she may be a candidate for medication. In Michigan, as a clinical psychologist, I cannot prescribe antidepressants, but I can refer her to a psychiatrist or to her own physician for an evaluation. However, I may not bring this up in the first session. Often light depression gives way as therapy progresses and deepens. Also, I find that many people are resistant to the mention of medication, feeling it to be an admission of weakness. So, while that is a thought in the back of my mind, unless the person is truly unable to function at present, that subject is tabled until I know her better.

As the session draws to a close, I ask how she feels about our meeting and if she would like to continue. If the feeling is mutually positive, then we make arrangements for future appointments. If she is uncertain, I don't push her to return, but offer to be available when she decides.

The first meeting is unlike any other because of the tension of a new relationship. If rapport is successful, however, the tension fades somewhere in the middle of the session. Then both of us can concentrate on the business at hand with a greater level of comfort in our newly forming bond.

Doctor, How Long Will This Take?

One of the first things a client wants to know is "How long?" *How long will I have to see you? How long will I feel this miserable? How long until I feel better? How long until I can spend my lunch hour eating instead of rushing here and back to work? How long until I can spend my money on something more fun than therapy?* It is a fair question, "How long?" and one which is very difficult to answer.

There are schools of psychotherapy which believe that it takes at least seven years for a patient (those schools have patients, not clients) to be ready to leave therapy. "At least" means that some stay much longer. That is often two or three sessions a week, without breaks except for the therapist's vacations. At the other end of the spectrum are newer strategies of brief therapy, taught at workshops all over the country. They emphasize limited ways to effectively help a client in perhaps six to eight visits, staying within the parameters set by managed care companies.

Those are the extremes. In between are the many people who came to see me anywhere from three months to three or four years, sometimes with time out to integrate what they had learned, and then returned to take one more step. With people who came in concerned about time, money and becoming dependent upon me or therapy itself, I often made short-term contracts: "Let's say you will come for six sessions, and then we will review what you have done and see if there is something else you feel is unfinished." At the end of the six weeks, they had a better idea of what the process was about, and were willing to renegotiate: "I'll continue until just before Christmas. Maybe by then I can be with my parents without getting angry at everything they say to me." Then, at the last session before Christmas, we might schedule a follow-up for some time in January, so that the client could report with pride about how well she did, and we could bring our work to a formal closure.

Conversely, the holiday with the family might have stirred up negative or painful childhood memories, and the client might come back in January saying, "I need to get at the root of this anger, because I think it has to do with how I was treated as a kid. It interferes with all my relationships." Then we are off for a new round, one where the work may be really productive because the motivation is coming from the client, and she is really invested in the process.

Somewhere between seven weeks and seven years lies a reasonable average. I worked with many people from one to three years, depending on the issues presented.

Why does psychotherapy take so long? There are a number of reasons.

To begin with, it often takes time for the real issue to emerge. Sometimes the client recognizes the underlying problem but is not ready to face it (her marriage is a sham, or her husband is physically abusive) or she needs to feel more trusting of the therapist before she can admit to it. Often, however, the client doesn't even know what the true issue is. "I'm here because I feel anxious a lot," a man tells me in our first session. "Especially at work."

"What do you think the anxiety is about?" I ask.

"Haven't got a clue," he replies.

I may not have a clue, either, when he first walks in. First I need to gather some background information. "How long have you experienced this anxiety at work? Where else do you feel this way? How long has this been the case?" I need information about his current living situation, his current relationships and his life outside of his job. I also need to find out about his family of origin. Are his parents still living? His siblings? How does he/did he get along with each of them? Has he been in therapy previously? Any addictions? I need to know about his state of health and about his hopes and aspirations, if he has any.

It may take more than one session for me to form a picture of this man in the context of his life. It may take three sessions, or three months. Material may emerge later, after he feels more trusting in our relationship. He may purposely conceal information that he feels uncomfortable about, or he may be unaware that what he is omitting is important in alleviating the distress he came in with. For instance, he may not want to tell me that his father beat him when he was a child, because he feels shame about these memories, or because he has convinced himself it is unimportant since he now gets along okay with his dad.

The client may not be aware that the roots of his present difficulty lie in the past. He also may not be interested in pursuing this path. He just wants a quick solution to the present dilemma. We make a working agreement toward reaching his goal. I can teach him some breathing and visualization techniques to use when his anxiety is high, as well as instruct him about the value of daily exercise and helpful inner dialogue, and send him on his way. In this case, the treatment may be short term, lasting anywhere from six weeks to six months.

I make clear to the client, however, that we are only dealing with surface symptoms. "If you feel more at ease and function better, this may be enough," I might tell him. "But if the anxiety continues, you are free to return for another round of exploration." It is my belief that the choice belongs to him. At the same time, I try to impart enough information so that his choice is an educated one.

"You say that your boss reminds you at times of your father," I reflect to the man who wants to terminate therapy sooner than I think is useful. "When you feel ready to explore your relationship with your father, you may find that your reaction to your boss will not feel so charged with anxiety." If he is unwilling to do that now, I honor his wishes and send him on his way to practice his new stress reduction techniques. He will decide for himself when he is ready to do longer-term therapy.

Most difficulties develop over time, and they need time to evolve in their resolution, as well. New patterns of behavior and of thinking may need to be practiced by the client and monitored by the therapist. A client may learn a new way of thinking or behaving, but it takes time to put it into practice, and even to recognize when it is appropriate to put it into practice. Old habits don't change in one session. I may find myself mentoring or coaching a woman as she learns to stand firm in the face of her husband's sarcasm. Standing firm is a new behavior for her and one she is not yet ready to take on without some back-up in therapy. Beneath a current issue (such as the sarcastic or emotionally abusive spouse) there may be a lifetime of similar issues (such as abusive parents) that take time to be explored. Brief therapy has to ignore these issues in order to stay brief.

Some people arrive at my door with a long road of therapy behind them and the likelihood that a long road exists ahead as well. These are often souls who were so badly damaged in childhood that it takes much of their adult lives to learn how to live in the world. Others come in because they are reacting to a traumatic event in the present: death of a loved one, a life-threatening illness, an unexpected job loss as their company downsized. For a person who was well-functioning before the traumatic life event, therapy may be helpful in very few sessions. Often in such situations I invite the person to return for a "check-in" a month hence, to see if his gains are holding and to determine whether there is more work to be done. Even after a mutually agreed upon closure, the door is always open if he wishes to return.

One other very basic factor enters into "how long" and that is financial. A weekly psychotherapy session is not an inexpensive commitment. It helps greatly when one's insurance covers this service. Often, however, only a certain number of sessions are covered per year. Then the client must pay out-of-pocket. Some people, unable to afford to pay, end their treatment and return the following year, when the insurance is again active. Others, who are truly engaged in the process and can manage the payment, opt to continue. Ending for financial reasons when the psychological work is not finished is unfortunate, but sometimes necessary. It is helpful for the therapist to anticipate this decision and discuss it with the client in advance of the insurance running out, so that plans can be made for keeping the gains that have been made and for the possibility of returning in the future.

While there is no simple or single answer to *Doctor, how long,* those who have stayed long enough to feel better and make positive life changes will usually tell you that the expenditure of time and money was definitely worth it.

It's Not My Decision

A woman comes to see me. She has been married for twenty years and the last ten have felt very empty. There is no relationship between herself and her husband any longer, she tells me, but the children are still in high school and are close to both parents. She can't stand being in the marriage but feels terrible guilt about disrupting the family with divorce. She wants me to tell her what to do.

A young man who is very handsome and successful in his business life has a dilemma he feels unable to resolve. He is in love with two women. Each one has given him an ultimatum: "Get rid of the other relationship before Christmas or I'm outta here." It is now December 1. He wants me to decide for him.

I have 35 clients. Every one of them has a life changing decision to make. Every one comes in hoping that I will make the decision for them. They *know* I won't, but they *hope* I will. They want to end the constant anxiety that comes from being in despair, in limbo, from not knowing what to do, from living in an untenable situation. They feel helpless. They feel like children. The child wants Mom to say "Yes" or "No" and take away the responsibility. They want to hear an Authority Figure tell them, "Marry this one. Divorce that one. Take this job. Have another baby."

But I won't do it. I cannot do it. I am so happy I do not have to do it. I will not play that role. I will not make decisions for other people's lives.

Even if I did, they would not accept my words. Their anxiety would not go away. The decision would not be real. In their own minds, the situation would not have been resolved.

Instead, I help them explore. We explore the realities of the external situation: *What would happen if you chose situation A? Situation B? How would you feel in each case? What would be the consequences?* We explore the history of decision-making in their life: *What other life situations presented you with such choices? How would your parents (alive or not, it doesn't matter) feel with either choice?* We explore the belief systems that prevent them from being decisive: *Whatever I do is wrong; God will never forgive me if I get a divorce; it's dangerous to make a mistake.* We listen to thoughts from parts of their minds they have been unaware of: an adolescent part that believes, *Dad doesn't like me to be better than him*; an inner child who longs for closeness but fears it, because being close meant being hurt.

The exploration can take a few weeks, or a few months. Or, in some cases, a few years. Meanwhile, life is moving on, and the other players in the person's life may leave, or stay, and take the decision away from him. Throughout all our explorations is the plea, hidden or overt, *Tell me what I should do.*

That is fine for a media psychologist or a lonely hearts columnist to do. It is not the role of a psychotherapist. My job is to help my client know more of herself, know what she wants, and be able to act effectively in the world.

But sometimes I wish I were a talk-show guru. It is so tempting, so gratifying to one's ego to be seen as the Person of Wisdom. It's fun to be paid for being an oracle (with no refunds if the advice turns out to be wrong). It is self-satisfying (and also self-deceptive, but we'll ignore that) to see oneself as knowing the answers for everyone else. "Get a divorce," I would say to this one, and "Stay married," to that one. "Marry this woman," I would tell the young man. "Ditch the other one."

But are there not times when it is appropriate to give direct advice? Yes. When a situation is abusive or otherwise dangerous, I don't wait six months for the client to get beaten up to figure out that she has to leave. When a child is in jeopardy, the therapist does not hesitate to act to protect her; in fact, we are required by law to report the situation. But for existential life decisions that are major but not life threatening, usually involving work or relationships, my job is to help my client reach his own decision.

There are such subtle ways I can abuse that power. I may refuse to give a direct opinion, but you may read it in the expression on my face, the look of shock in my eyes, or a small smile that indicates that I agree with you. I can ask loaded questions, like a clever cross examiner trying a case, that lead you to an inevitable conclusion, although it may not be the conclusion you would reach if I asked you a different way. I can say to a young wife who suspects, but does not know, that her husband has another woman in his life, *"Why do you believe him when he says he is working late at the office?"* and thus plant suspicion in her mind. I can say, *"Why do you want to stay married to him when he talks to you like that?"* Enough questions like this can convince the young wife that she ought to file for divorce: never mind that I don't know if he really is working late; if her report of how he talks to her is accurate; what she might say or do, that she hasn't told me about, to goad him into angry behavior; the effect on their young children if the family is broken up. The therapist must be very mindful of the wording and tone of questions which can lead a client to think in one direction and overlook another.

The above questions, in and of themselves, might be appropriate to ask in some situations. They might be prefaced with "Let me play devil's advocate here. Tell me why you believe him," and, later, "why you doubt him." And, "How might you determine what is true?"

A therapist may, in some circumstances, give an opinion. It should be stated clearly as, "This is how I see your situation, and this is my sense of the action you should take; if you do not, this is what I fear as a possible consequence." This is most appropriate if a person is coming for a one-time consultation and has indicated that he wants a professional opinion on an issue. Even then, however, it must be offered as an opinion based on the information given, not as a dictum to take action. It is one more piece of evidence for the client to weigh in making his own decision, finally, about which road to travel.

If I am driving in a new area and get lost, I stop for directions. The man at the service station may show me a map and say "There are two ways to get there. I would take this one because it's faster. The other road is much prettier but slower, and may have some construction."

As I drive away, the choice is mine. I don't want to offer less to my clients.

My Sacred Ten Minutes

The attractive, well-dressed young woman dashes into my office breathless, fifteen minutes late.

"Oh, I'm so sorry," she apologizes. "I overslept, and then there was an accident on I-75 that closed two lanes, and…"

I motion to the chairs waiting for us. "Let's just get started," I say gently.

"Yes, but I hope I haven't thrown off your schedule…" she begins again.

"Of course not," I remind her. "It's just that we will have less time today to work together. We still must end at the same time."

Her face falls, and then she remembers. She knew that, but had forgotten. We spend much of the session on the issue of her lack of punctuality in many situations, and explore how that does and does not serve her. By the end of the shorter session she is beginning to understand that arriving late has something to do with her sense of powerlessness and control issues. She sees that this is connected, somehow, to what she had really wanted to talk about, her relationship with her boyfriend. She leaves my office on time and I have my sacred ten minutes before the next session begins.

One of the boundaries I establish in the first session is time. Sessions begin on the hour and end by ten minutes before the next hour. No exceptions, unless a double session has been negotiated in advance. This ten minute break is essential to me for several purposes: writing notes, clearing my mind, and focusing briefly on the next client.

Writing notes can be a chore, or can be simplified. I find it essential to take the simple route. As soon as this client leaves, I enter my notes: "Came 15 min. late. Explored lateness as a control issue. Hmwk: notice her own thoughts as she prepares to meet someone." I write my notes immediately because by the end of the day I sometimes do not recall easily the contents of each session (a mental flaw of aging, perhaps). Since the notes are mainly for my own benefit, I abbreviate words because I am in a hurry. (Although insurance companies require notes, in 25 years I never had anyone check mine.) I eliminate details because knowing the topic (punctuality) brings to my mind all the conversation we had; I don't need to write more. I use "lateness" rather than "unpunctuality" because it is easier to spell and comes to me more readily as I write. I include the homework assignment so I will remember to pick up on it the next time we meet. The entire note takes less than a minute to write. As I replace the file in the drawer I feel a sense of closure for that session.

(Note: if I had to write notes for Blue Cross, which sometimes did audits and actually might send someone to read the notes, I was required to follow a different formula, called SOAP: Subjective (what the client experienced), Objective (what I observed), Action (what we did in the session) and Prognosis (what comes next). In that case I would write: S: Feeling guilty about being late. O: agitated and apologetic. A: explored control issues in relationship to tardiness. P: shows ability for insight; needs to relate this to relationship issues in future sessions. The "P" entry establishes that her therapy needs to continue.)

When I re-file my last client's folder, I also pull out the folder for the next client and briefly glance at my notes from the prior session. Then I stand up, stretch, perhaps take a bathroom break or, occasionally, pour myself a cup of coffee. Returning to my office, I shut the door and sit quietly for a moment, focused on the coming session. My brief notes from last week are helpful in quickly replaying this man's story, his conflicts, his goals, and my next steps in facilitating change. I close my eyes and take a deep breath. I hold the thought that this will be a session helpful to him, one in which I am able to listen deeply and help him to go deep as well.

Then I open my eyes, straighten the papers on my desk, open the door and invite my next client to come in. My ten minutes has been essential to my work and to my own sense of well-being.

If the therapist is to have ten minutes free between clients, a practical issue is how to end a session on time. I begin to make closing remarks about five minutes before the client needs to walk out the door. "It's almost time to stop," I might say, "why don't we start next week with the question you just raised." Or, "There is something useful you might do between now and your appointment next week." Or, "How did you feel about this session?" and, "Do you want to come in next week or wait two weeks this time?" (This type of question is for someone who is winding down his work, and validates that he is getting close to his goal.) Along with one of these transitional remarks, I might shift in my chair, as if preparing to rise. The client then follows suit, and the session ends on time.

My use of time is not always so ideal. Sometimes a session runs over, and the next client walks in just as the last one has left, and I begin without the closure of writing my notes for the session just completed. At the beginning of those hours, I often find that while I am outwardly attentive, my mind is partly back in the last session. I am listening, but not as deeply tuned in as I need to be for optimal helpfulness. Images of a tragic story I have just been told are flashing through my awareness, or regret that I had neglected to state something with more clarity. If I have not taken time to review last week's file for the second client, I am also less focused at first. Although I quickly bring myself into connection with the person sitting in front of me, I have lost something in the first five minutes, and I feel less settled.

I recall answering an ad once for a clinic near my home that had office space and was hiring therapists. When they told me that I would be expected to have 45 minute sessions "back to back" (with no time in between) so that four people could be seen in two hours time, I knew I could not work there. I was acquainted with many therapists who loved to say things like, "I saw ten people yesterday, back to back." Their tone always made me want to ask the old question, "Are you bragging or complaining?"

I needed that short time between sessions. It might be more efficient monetarily to work "back to back," but for me it was less efficient psychologically, and that was all that mattered.

But I Can't Be Your Friend

"Thank you," the young woman says to me, with tears in her eyes, as she is about to walk out the door. "You have been so helpful. I think of you not as a counselor but as a friend."

Yikes! She has it all wrong. I'm not a friend. This is a professional relationship. There is a difference, a big difference.

But I can't say that now. I hear her with my heart, and she is truly expressing gratitude. This is not the moment to get picky. I can clarify it all when she comes back. Next week I will be able to explain to her the unique nature of the therapeutic relationship. I will tell her that it differs from a "friendship" in many ways, even when I am being very friendly.

For one thing, this is not a two-way relationship. The balance is tipped: she is the seeker and I am the guide. In a friendship, we would trade roles back and forth. This week she tells me her troubles, next week I tell her mine.

That is not the case in psychotherapy.

In a friendship, we would see each other in a variety of locations, such as "out to lunch" or shopping or walking or going to the movies, or visiting at each other's homes. But not here. This is strictly office business. There are definite boundaries, and they are not to be crossed.

In a friendship, we might call each other at any time and talk for unspecified stretches. In therapy, I set definite parameters around phone calls: call my office, not my home; ask a specific question and I will offer as specific an answer as possible; I limit calls to two or three minutes; I do not do therapy by phone. And I do not phone my clients except to change appointment times or inquire after an emergency situation. Even then, I usually ask them to call me.

I respond differently as a therapist than as a friend. At least, I used to: the therapist in me is now so much a part of me that I may respond as a therapist with my friends. But not the reverse. The difference is in the depth with which I listen and the way I keep the focus. In a social conversation, I may be the one to lose the focus, or to switch it from my friend's situation to my own. My friends understand: they do the same thing.

As a friend, I engage in social chit-chat. As a therapist, I try to avoid that as much as possible.

As a friend, I am available whenever I am needed. As a therapist, I am available during scheduled appointments.

As a friend, our focus together has to do with sharing aspects of our lives. As a therapist, our focus has to do with helping you see your behavior from a different perspective.

As a friend, I accept you the way you are and do not try to "help" you to change. As a therapist, my defined goal is to help you bring change to your life. I start with accepting you the way you are, but if our time together is devoted to helping you stay that way, you are wasting our time and your money.

As a friend, I can be as informal and silly as I wish to be. As a psychotherapist, I feel some constraints to act professional, to take you and our work together seriously.

So, regardless of how friendly and supportive I may be toward you, I am not here to be a girlfriend to you. That would be a diminishment of what I have to offer.

I plan to make this very clear to my client at the next session.

Except that she has left a phone message saying she does not feel the need to come back since I helped her so much and she would like to call me some time so we can go out for coffee.

PART II

The Business of Private Practice

How I Built a Practice

As I am hanging up the phone, my office partner stops by my door to tell me her happy news. Her daughter has just been accepted to a doctoral program in clinical psychology. My friend's excitement causes me to reflect on the years when I entered this field. Many things have changed. There are more hurdles today than when I was starting out. Training, academic expectations and licensing requirements are more rigorous. The world my friend's daughter is entering may appear more professional, but I wonder whether it will be as much fun.

◆　　◆　　◆

In the beginning, I had a Master's Degree in Education and a background in public school teaching. I had participated enthusiastically in all sorts of groups that were wildly popular in the 1970's: sensitivity groups, personal growth groups, encounter groups, Transactional Analysis (TA) groups and weekend marathons. I knew that I had the interest and the skills to be a group leader. I didn't know how to find groups to lead.

I first found my answer when I signed up for a year-long training program in TA. The program led to certification as a TA leader. It required that each member find a way to obtain group-leading experience using the TA model of therapy. Since I was not yet a mental health professional, I had no clinic or job to fall back on. Instead, I was invited to join a social worker who was organizing groups where she worked and wanted a co-leader. That was my first experience on the "professional" side. I loved the work and my co-leader and I began a life-long friendship. My hours in the TA training group and the work I did as a co-leader enabled me to be granted a CSW (certified social worker) status with the State of Michigan.

The TA training program encouraged people to go into their communities and teach TA theory wherever they could. I found a niche at a local community adult education program. My classes, like the earlier groups of which I had been a member, were experiential, providing opportunities for participants to understand theory by applying it to their own lives. This began a process of change which many people wanted to continue. I provided that opportunity by organizing small TA groups at a private office which I shared with another trainee who was doing the same thing.

These groups were the start of my private practice, although at the time I didn't think of it that way. I was simply, in the jargon of the day, "doing group." Each group was run like a class, a set fee for a set number of weeks, usually eight. If enough members of the group wanted to continue, we set up another eight week schedule. Occasionally people who had dropped out of the group asked to meet with me privately.

One day, I realized I had enough clients to join a private mental health clinic. Being part of a clinic had several advantages: I felt less isolated professionally; I could use the clinic resources to send out insurance statements; there were meetings to discuss clinical issues and the psychiatrist who owned the clinic occasionally referred clients to me. Clients referred their friends, family and colleagues to me, as well. My practice began to build.

I had wanted merely to lead groups and along the way I had become a psychotherapist. I attended every kind of psychotherapy conference and training that was available in my area and felt comfortable with my work. I did not, however, feel comfortable about my academic degree, now that I was committed to a new profession. By the end of the 1970's, Michigan laws were tightening up regarding licensing and insurance payments. I decided I would like to have a PhD in clinical psychology, but I wanted a program with an orientation that was humanistic rather than analytic, and did not know where I would find one. By serendipity, just at that time a colleague told me about a new doctoral program in Detroit. He was completing his own work there and highly recommended that I check it out. I did, and found it was exactly what I was looking for. It was headed by Dr. Clark Moustakas and Dr. Cereta Perry, early pioneers in the field of humanistic psychology.

In fall of 1979, when my youngest child left for college, I began my doctoral studies. Three days every week I drove to my office to see clients, left at 11:30 am and jumped in my car to race down the freeway from the suburb where I worked to Detroit, where my classes were. Often I ate lunch while I was driving: a peanut butter and jelly sandwich, or a bagel with cream cheese. By noon I was seated in a small circle with nine other students, six of them considerably younger than myself, ready to explore whatever was on the agenda that day: diagnostic testing, existential philosophy as applied to psychotherapy, humanistic practices in the classroom, alternative methods such as art, music and poetry therapy, phenomenological research, and group process. (Like a kaleidoscope, the process changes in every group, so however much one studies it, it always is different.)

The sessions were lively and stimulating. We did not simply learn theory in the abstract; rather, we were encouraged to filter it through our own experience and to use what we were learning as we interacted with clients.

Added to my already busy schedule was an internship in clinical psychology, separate from my own practice, where I received excellent training and supervision. Once again, my contacts led to the referral of new clients, particularly from my internships (there were two, each one lasting a year). One internship was at the psychology clinic of a local university. Several clients I met there as young students continued their work with me after they graduated and had new issues to resolve in their adult lives.

Once I had completed all the requirements for my PhD and for State licensure as a psychologist, I noticed an increase in the number of referrals that came from acquaintances in other professions, such as attorneys and medical doctors. Not only did I have four more years of solid professional experience, but I think I exuded more confidence when I spoke about my work.

◆   ◆   ◆

As I think back about how I began, I realize that I did things in reverse order from how they would be done today by first building a practice, then obtaining the academic training and fulfilling internship requirements. Yet, the things I did to increase my practice are still applicable for my friend's daughter or anyone else who chooses to go into private practice: first, complete your academic work, internships and whatever requirements for licensing your state requires. Next, get your name and your face in front of the public by giving talks, teaching adult education classes or offering one-day workshops. Tell colleagues you are open for referrals. Contact people you know in other professions. Attend professional meetings and be active in their networks. Consider writing a column for a local paper or newsletter. Each time you move to a new location, send announcements to everyone you know. Develop a specialty and let everyone know about it. Most of all, be effective: when others see how your clients have improved their lives, they will ask for your name. To steal a line from the movie "Field of Dreams," *If you build it, they will come.*

The Setting

So that you, the reader, can envision the stories told here in a specific setting, I will invite you to my final office, the one where I lived happily for the longest single period of time.

My particular room was part of a suite which I shared harmoniously with two other psychologists, women who were both colleagues and good friends. We shared in common the area that was the waiting room. All of us agreed that we wanted the immediate feeling, when a client first entered, to be one of comfort. We chose wicker furniture and soft shades of mauve and cream for the carpet, the furniture, the cushions on the chairs and a large print on the wall facing the door. A bulletin board held announcements of community meetings, such as AA or parenting groups, as well as lectures, concerts, seminars and any other material that might be of interest to our clients. A radio played classical music and there were magazines to browse through, everything from *New Age Journal* and *Institute of Noetic Sciences Bulletin* (my contributions) to *Time*, *People Magazine*, and *Monthly Detroit* (my colleagues' choices). We were an eclectic group.

When we first rented the suite, we had to decide which office would belong to whom. The three rooms were different sizes and shapes, and had features that were both plusses and minuses for each of us. This turned out to be a very easy decision, however: Gayle, the only coffee drinker among us, wanted to be in the room closest to the small "kitchen" area, where the coffeepot was. Sara liked the middle office, which was considerably larger than the others. I was immediately drawn to the smallest room, in spite of its size, because it was the farthest from the waiting area, affording the most privacy, and because of the number of windows. We did not have to debate, draw straws, or resort to fisticuffs. This was, incidentally, a pleasant foreshadowing of how peaceful together our association proved to be, for all the years we were together.

Please come into my office now. Stretching to our left is a rectangular room, with the doorway in the right hand corner. Facing us is an entire wall of windows, four of them, floor to ceiling. They have mini-blinds which allow in the light but afford privacy in the rare event that someone is outside the building. The windows overlook a grassy area, with trees, on the side of the building.

Beyond the grass is a sidewalk which is seldom used by anyone; beyond that, a narrow strip of lawn, and a two lane street with minimal traffic during most of the day. The windows actually open, in contrast to the sleek, sealed in offices in newer buildings. Fresh air and light are two important priorities for me, and I feel happy in this room because of the windows.

As we enter my office, facing into the short wall on the right is the desk, a sturdy oak, which has changed locations with me for many years. On the desk is a telephone, the normal, old fashioned kind, with push-button dialing and no other fancy gadgets, and a separate, very small answering machine. There is a battery operated clock, with easy-to-read numerals, which can be moved around the office as needed. Wedged into the space between the end of the desk and the windows is a file cabinet. Facing the desk is a comfortable chair on wheels.

Against the short wall to the extreme left of the rectangular room is a small sofa, light denim-blue with white piping. The color, against the mauve carpet, feels soothing to me. Adjacent to the sofa, in a deeper tone of the same blue, are two small, light weight barrel chairs, which face each other, and can easily be moved around as needed. On either side, back against the wall, are two large floor cushions, and on the window side, a floor lamp. Other than the barrel chair with its back to the window, there is no furniture blocking the windows, only a grouping of plants, usually including fresh mums, on the floor along that wall.

A blue and white striped futon is folded on the floor on the long wall facing the windows. On top of it are two throw pillows and a white teddy bear. Angled into the farthest corner of that wall is a tall bookcase, in the same oak as the desk. On the wall are five photographs, three of the Grand Canyon and two of Mt. Rainier, which I shot with my Nikon on trips with my husband.

I generally sit in the chair that faces the windows. I prefer that I be the one distracted by the outside, rather than interfering with my clients' concentration. Also, since I am in the office many hours at a time, I feel less closed in when I can face the outer view. When someone comes in for the first time, I point out my chair (or perhaps have my appointment book and glasses on it) and invite the other person to take a seat anywhere else, which could be the other chair, the sofa or the floor. Once a client who was chronically afraid to try anything new suggested that we trade seats: she would face the window, and I could sit elsewhere. It was a sign of progress for her to initiate a new pattern, and I readily agreed. That was how I discovered that even facing the wall had its distractions: the light from the windows behind me reflected into the glass on the framed photographs, turning them into mirrors. I could see the outside traffic as it passed. We had some amused discussion of the relative merits of the distractions in both positions. It was a good experiment, but at the next session she resumed her old favorite position, stretched out on the sofa with her back to the windows.

The futon is also available, although seldom chosen on a first visit. This is a long, down-filled cushion that folds into thirds. Folded, it provides a seat; opened, it is a comfortable floor mat. It is often used when someone is learning progressive relaxation, deep breathing techniques, or re-experiencing painful memories and emotions from childhood. Over the years, it was my experience that fewer and fewer clients were willing to become vulnerable enough to stretch out on the mat to sob or have a temper tantrum, as happened routinely in my training groups in the '70's and early '80's. I explained and invited, but never pushed or otherwise insisted on the more expressive forms of therapy. The futon increasingly became decorative rather than functional. People improved in therapy all the same.

The narrow bookcase in the corner holds a number of psychotherapy texts. There is also a stack of issues of "The American Psychologist," most of which I have glanced through but not read. At the end of the year I throw them away and collect a new pile. The bottom half of the bookcase has two deep shelves concealed by a door, where I store necessary supplies such as extra boxes of Kleenex and light bulbs.

My office is a relatively quiet place, although I cannot keep out all intrusive sound. Occasionally a fire truck screams by, or a workman hammers on the outside of the building. That simply has to be tolerated. The insulation between my office and the other rooms of the suite is good: I seldom hear the voices of others, and sounds within my office generally don't carry beyond my walls. Even my phone is quiet: I keep the ringer turned off during sessions, as well as the volume on the answering machine. Aside from two clicks when a call comes in (I never answer when I am in session), the only sounds are the voices of myself and my client.

My office gives me pleasure. It is my hope that the physical environment provides an aura of calmness and safety for others, to balance the tumultuous emotions and raw pain carried by most of those who enter the room.

Diagnosis and Managed Care

A man in his 50's walks into my office. He is unable to function well in his life. He has trouble holding jobs, making conversation, even forcing himself to take a shower. He has no family and few friends. Yet he seems to be intelligent, kind, concerned about the fate of the world, pleasant in his general demeanor. When he is alone, he sculpts animals in clay. Currently, he is working at an office supply store and has healthcare coverage. He has come to see me because his loneliness and anxiety are unbearable.

As I listen to the story of his tormented childhood, I begin to understand the forces that shape his way of viewing the world. I see the creative child still active behind the socially withdrawn adult. I see a complex human, vulnerable and defended, immobilized but longing to change, isolated yet wanting a fuller existence. I do not see a label.

Yet, in order for him to be reimbursed by his insurance company, I must provide them with the essence of his soul summed up into a diagnostic category with a number and a name. I have several choices. For this man, I could select "general depressive disorder" or "generalized anxiety disorder," which are the two least pejorative labels. I could choose "post-traumatic stress disorder," since most of his under-functioning resulted from a traumatized childhood at the hands of his abusive father. I could also label him with "anti-social personality disorder," reflecting his difficulty making friends. Yet, all of these labels seem irrelevant as I sit face to face with this hurting soul. When I speak to him, I envision a life span that began in a pain-filled childhood and continued into a dysfunctional adulthood and yet, simultaneously, I also see this man as holding the potential to change, to become something other, something more, than how he appears at this moment. My task is to help him to expand his own vision. What we do in each session begins with what he brings with him that day: his demeanor, emotional state, the content of his words, the situations he presents. The work is not dependent upon the diagnostic code.

In theory, each diagnostic code suggests an approach to treatment. If the diagnosis is "depression," then I must take steps to treat the depression. If it is "anti-social personality disorder," my work with him would have a different focus.

31

Each category is a lens the therapist peers through. At times this is helpful. I need to recognize his depression, for example, in order to recommend that he have a psychiatric evaluation for appropriate medication. Diagnostic categories follow the medical model of psychotherapy: someone is ill, there are identifiable symptoms, the symptoms fit into a diagnostic category, knowing the diagnosis aids in choosing the treatment.

Sometimes, however, emphasizing the diagnosis is like looking at a beautiful landscape through a knothole in a wooden fence. A certain amount of the scene is within range, but the rest is blotted out. The big picture is missing. This talented, sensitive man extends far beyond his depression. It is not helpful for either one of us to regard him only as a "depressive" and ignore the rest.

In my humanistic training, in the 1970's, labels were de-emphasized. We were encouraged to see the whole person: his longings, aspirations, values, what gave meaning to his life. We were taught to see the human being beyond his symptoms. Many of my mentors and colleagues derided the medical model that required diagnostic categories. "People are too complex," they said. "They don't fit into little boxes with labels. The labels are dehumanizing." Some of them opted to simply charge less and ignore insurance reimbursements.

By the 1980's, when I was affiliated with various clinics, it was clear to me that I had to make some sort of diagnosis if people were to be able to benefit from their insurance coverage. Diagnostic categories are contained in a book known as the Diagnostic and Statistical Manual (DSM), written by members of the American Psychiatric Association (APA), and now into its 4th edition (DSM IV). Each category and sub-category has a name, a number and a description. Every few years a new version is published, often invalidating the carefully chosen labels of the previous years.

Often I searched through this book and could not find an accurate description of someone I was treating. Sometimes a client appeared to fit into many categories at once. Some of the diagnoses appeared to me to carry a social stigma. This was particularly true of one label, homosexuality, which, thankfully, has been removed because it is no longer considered pathology. Another, Multiple Personality Disorder, has now been renamed Dissociative Identity Disorder. I imagined a person applying for a new job with new insurance and having these pejorative labels pop up on someone's computer, and I froze. Making a diagnosis felt like a breach of the principles of confidentiality. Years ago there was a category labeled "Adjustment to Adult Life," which seemed to be the most innocuous one in the book. That, however, was eliminated shortly after I discovered its usefulness. My more experienced colleagues advised me to stick with "Depression" and "Anxiety" as the two basic diagnostic categories. Almost everyone experiences one or the other; there is no great stigma attached. Yet no label ever seemed to capture the essence of the complex, vulnerable men and women who faced me weekly in my office.

The theory behind using diagnoses, or the medical model, is that the psychotherapist must know what is wrong to do proper treatment. This is both true and not-true. If a client does not appear depressed but only complains of being tired, I might erroneously encourage her to get more sleep instead of steering her toward getting more exercise and daylight, or seeing a psychiatrist for the proper antidepressant. However, if I regard her only as a "depressive personality," I may lower my vision of who she can become, and thus contribute to keeping her "stuck" in a labeled box.

As the use of managed care has increased, diagnosis has become a crucial issue. Many managed care companies limit the number of sessions they will pay for a client within a given time period, based on the diagnosis. By the mid-'90's, dealing with managed care had become an irritating and intrusive ritual for me and my colleagues. The ritual goes something like this:

In order to continue treating my client, I have to obtain permission from a young social work graduate whose job is to save the company money. She doesn't know me or my client, or anything about the carefully constructed therapeutic relationship between us. She wants to know only the diagnosis, my goals, how I am carrying them out and what progress the person is making. She might also instruct me in how to do therapy with my client. Then this third-party stranger decides how many weeks of therapy are necessary.

To obtain permission to continue, I must be careful and creative in my presentation.

"Yes, my client has made great progress in overcoming her anxiety," I might say. "But now she needs to work on her relationship with her mother before they're together for Christmas. This is her next goal. It's the issue at the core of her depression and anger."

If I am successful, the case manager will allow another six weeks. Then the process must be repeated.

These phone calls take place during "normal business hours," which means that I have to squeeze them in between appointments or give up my lunch break. To make things more difficult, there is often a long telephone wait, listening to Musak or a commercial for the insurance company, until the case manager becomes available.

I found this system intrusive, frustrating, time-consuming and demeaning. Fortunately, I did not have too many clients with managed care policies until shortly before I closed down my practice. My colleagues told me, "You got out just in time!"

The Financial Side: Keeping it Simple

During the years that I worked at a variety of private clinics, many of my business needs were taken care of by an office staff. Someone else billed insurance companies, collected payments, took phone messages and kept my files. (I did my own scheduling, however.) The rooms were already furnished. All I had to do was show up and be with my clients. At the end of the month, the clinic paid me a percentage of the fees I had collected and kept the rest.

In those early days of my practice, I was required by Michigan law to be in a work setting that included a licensed psychologist and a psychiatrist on staff. Both were to have access to all my records and were required to schedule a certain number of hours of face-to-face supervision. This might have been very helpful, or it might have felt intrusive. The real truth, however, is that my records were never perused and supervision happened only when I asked for a consultation. I was quite happy with that system.

Eventually, I fulfilled the requirements of becoming a licensed psychologist myself. This entailed earning my PhD, working under supervision for two more years, and passing a State examination. I then had the option of moving out on my own. This presented me with a new set of choices as I became, in essence, a small business owner.

There are many ways to do the business of running a private practice. My goal in all instances was to keep it simple. I wanted to put my time and energy into helping my clients and not be distracted by a complicated structure. I also wanted to keep my expenses as low as possible.

To this end, I teamed up with a friend and colleague who was also newly licensed. Together we searched for and found space that accommodated two offices and a waiting room. It was in a building that was easily accessible to expressways and had good parking. Most important of all, the rent was low. If business faltered, we could still afford to be there.

Other than rent, my only other monthly expense was for the office telephone. That, too, was simple: just a basic line with no other services. I have never liked the forced rudeness of call waiting, although I use it on my home phone. Voice mail was not yet a phone company service; I used an answering machine.

My partner and I discussed having a receptionist and decided it was unnecessary. Our clients simply came into the waiting room and sat down. When it was time, we came to the waiting room to invite them in. Since each of us also had our own phone answering system and did our own billing, there was no need to have an extra person around. This decision eliminated the stress of interviewing, hiring and training an employee. It meant that the design of our office space could be simpler, since there was no need for an extra room for a receptionist/secretary. Most importantly, it eliminated a major monthly salary expense.

I handled the matter of fees in a very simple way: clients understood from the outset that they were to pay me at each session. I accepted checks or cash, but not credit cards, another simplification. One session, one check, just the way they handle things at the hair salon. Everyone understood and I never had a problem with this system. No one owed me money; no one built up a huge therapy debt to add to their other problems, and I had less to worry about.

Occasionally someone forgot his checkbook. I then could be magnanimous and say, "It's okay. Just drop a check in the mail before our next session." When I knew the client well enough, I might say, "Pay me at the next session." They almost always did. If someone owed me for more than two weeks, I simply didn't make another appointment until we had worked out a payment arrangement. If a client requested to pay monthly, I agreed—so long as it was for a month in advance. Sometimes that was the end of that request.

The rules were clear. My clients did not take financial advantage of me.

Most clients had insurance coverage. I asked that they pay me; then, at the end of the month, I gave each one a written statement with all the necessary data; they mailed it to their insurance company and were reimbursed. As with most of my rules, I made exceptions. In a very few situations, when the client absolutely had no expendable income and had a reliable insurance program, I billed the company directly each month and received a check within two weeks. For clients with Blue Cross/Blue Shield plans which paid for the first ten sessions but had more elaborate requirements than my simple handwritten statements, I turned over the paper work to a service that specialized in Blue Cross billing. The fee for this service was minimal.

At the end of each day, I recorded payments on a log sheet for each client, along with the date and time of the session. That was the extent of my bookkeeping. I didn't even use a computer. My bookkeeping system may have been primitive, but it worked. I took in more than I spent. I kept some of my income in an office checking account that was separate from my home account. I used the office account for all business related expenses, such as rent, psychology conferences, membership dues to professional organizations and licensing fees. That made it easy for my accountant and kept everything clear in case I was ever audited by the IRS (which never happened). I kept a necessary amount for personal use and the rest went into an IRA.

Psychotherapy is complex; finances were simple; life was good.

Dealing with No-shows

It is almost 3:00 pm. I have three more clients scheduled. I am thinking now about the woman who has made an appointment for 3:00. I review her file. I recall that when she left she had just brought up a new topic, and I suggested that we begin there at the next session. I am glad we have a starting point. I look forward to seeing her.

Soon it is 3:10, then 3:20. She has not arrived. She has not phoned, either. I wonder: *Was she in an accident? Did she forget? Did I write her appointment in the wrong slot? Can I leave the office to run an errand, or will she show up as soon as I have gone? How long should I wait? Why am I stuck in this room with this dilemma?*

At 3:25 I dial her number. She answers. She is so pleased to hear my voice! This is not good news. I say, "You're not supposed to be there; you're supposed to be in my office."

"Oh, no!" she says. "I thought our appointment was for tomorrow! Wait until I find your card…"

I wait.

"Oh," she says when she returns to the phone. "It was today, wasn't it! I'm so sorry. Can I come tomorrow instead?"

She can't because my schedule is full. We reschedule for the following week.

In the jargon of the therapy world, she is a "no-show."

When I hang up, I feel angry. I have been "stood up." There is not enough time left for me to leave the office, but too much time for me to spend waiting for the next appointment. On a day where my time is tightly scheduled, in a life where my time is carefully managed, this is a wasted hour.

According to the rules of the therapy business, it is acceptable to charge "no-shows" for the missed hour. There are good reasons for this. First, not coming to the session is sometimes an unconscious statement of resistance on the part of the client. In reserving an hour and not showing up, a silent statement is made, equally as relevant to the therapy as a verbal one in person. Therefore, not being present is still considered a session. A second rationale is that charging for a missed session establishes who sets the rules. If the therapist is not in charge of the ground rules of therapy, he is open to manipulation and the treatment is not going to be effective. Thirdly, charging for a missed session is a protection for the therapist. With no fee, the therapist could be a prisoner all day, closed in a room, waiting, while no one comes. This gives the clients power that is non-therapeutic for them and enraging to the therapist, which is not at all helpful to the therapeutic relationship.

Charging a fee for unused sessions gives the proper message that making an appointment is serious business and that time should be respected. Many years ago, I went to a hairdresser who had a little hand printed sign in his mirror that read, "Broken appointments must be paid for." Just the thought of paying for a haircut I didn't receive made me sure to never forget my appointment with him.

But there is a catch to this. A therapy appointment is much more expensive than a haircut and is usually paid for, totally or partially, by the insurance company. However, insurance cannot be charged, legally, if the patient isn't actually there. That is called "insurance fraud," and we often read about that in the newspaper, when the doctor is arrested and taken to jail.

That means the client is liable for the fee out of her own pocket.

Wait a minute! I hear you saying. *You mean that if the client comes for a session, it is "free" (since the insurance covers it) but if she doesn't come, there is a $100.00 or more out-of-pocket fee? That's a bit steep, isn't it? Is that meant to be a punishment for bad behavior? Is that therapeutic? And what about human error? Haven't you sometimes forgotten an appointment, or written it down for the wrong time, or scheduled two people at the same time, or not remembered to meet a friend for lunch, or...?*

Once, at a meeting of an organization of women psychologists, the speaker asked a group of about 60 women, most with PhD's, to raise their hands if they had a policy of charging for no-shows. All the hands went up. Then she instructed, "Raise your hand if you consistently enforce that policy." Only three or four hands went up. Everyone laughed sheepishly. The speaker revealed that in the clinic where she worked, every therapist, other than herself, charged *every* client for *every* session that was not canceled with 24 hours notice. It so happened, she told us, that all the other therapists were male. (This is not intended to be a sexist statement; I'm merely reporting what was said.)

A lively discussion ensued. Various reasons were given, all of which I could identify with, as to why the women were not consistent in enforcing their own rule. A big one was compassion: the client was driving to the appointment and her tire blew out on the way. Or someone rear-ended her car while she was stopped at a red light. Or the baby sitter failed to show up and she would have to bring all four children with her, including the baby, who was teething and hadn't slept. The therapist has spent many sessions hearing about the financial difficulties of the family, and is privately thinking how fortunate she herself is to be leaving for a trip to Italy. So how can she charge this young mother, who now is without a car or a sitter, for something that is not her fault, when she herself can really afford to give up the cash? Or, the therapist remembers that she forgot her dentist appointment last week and was not charged.

If I charge, I feel guilty. If I do not, I feel resentful. This is the dilemma of the compassionate therapist. What is the way out?

This was my semi-resolution: at the first session, along with other information about the nature of therapy, fees and financial arrangements, I made it *very clear* that all appointments *must* be canceled within 24 hours (a call to my office machine at midnight was acceptable) to avoid paying a fee. I made it clear that the fee could not be charged to their insurance, that this was standard practice in my business, that it was not a punishment, that I did not want to be in the role of deciding whether or not the reason given for not coming was valid or not, and that late cancellation or not showing up at all left me with a blank hour that someone else needed but did not know about in time to utilize.

By the time my speech had ended, I had instilled fear of the wrath of the gods. The result was that very few clients defaulted without notice. When they did, they usually said, "And I'll send you a check for the hour." I accepted the check the first time, with just a little guilt, but with much gratitude for their willingness to comply. I wanted to establish that I am a woman of my word. If there was a second (or third) emergency (such as "I know we have a 10 o'clock appointment and it is 8:30, but I woke up vomiting and can't lift my head off the pillow except to stagger to the bathroom,") then I could afford to be magnanimous. When they came for the next appointment, I might say, "Just pay me your 50% co-pay, and I'll waive the rest *this time* because you were so ill." That way I only felt 50% as guilty.

The result of my clear policy was that I had very few clients who abused the 24 hour notice rule, and did not lose income because someone changed her mind about coming but neglected to tell me.

There was one situation, however, when it was not possible to charge for a no-show. That was when it was a first appointment, and the person never arrived.

In one such case, I received a call from a young man (at least, he sounded young on the phone). He wanted to know if I was qualified to help him with a very special problem. He told me he was a cross dresser and it was beginning to cause him some embarrassment. We made an appointment for the following week. I gave him careful directions to my office, and requested that he phone if he could not be there for some reason. He assured me he would do so. I thought this would be a most interesting case and decided to do some homework. I ran a computer check and found several recent articles about the etiology and treatment of cross dressing, ordered and read the articles carefully. I thought about how I would work with this young man in our first session.

The allotted time came. And went. I finished up some paper work, returned a couple of phone calls, and waited. He was my last appointment, and I was ready to go home to dinner. I was annoyed.

My partner was still in her office, and we met at the coffeepot when her client left. I unloaded my irritation to her always-empathic ears. This time, however, she looked astonished. "I'll bet that was the same guy who called me last week," she said. "Was his name John, and he didn't want to tell you his last name?"

It was, and he didn't. He had suckered both of us (and, we found out later, at least two other colleagues as well).

Those are the breaks. Meanwhile, I shared the articles with my friends. We all learned a lot, in case another cross-dresser phones one of us some day.

PART III

Listening: the Core of the Work

Creativity and Intuition

Early in my career, I attend a training session with a highly skilled psychotherapist from California who has been invited to the town where I live in Michigan. I volunteer to be one of the six participants in a simulated demonstration group. The six of us sit in a circle with the trainer, surrounded by the other eighty therapists who have signed up for this session.

I am startled when our trainer looks directly at me and states, "You had a grandfather who totally loved and doted on you."

Immediately the image of my mother's father, my beloved Grandpa Lou, fills my mind. All my grandparents loved me, as did my parents, but there was a special quality to this relationship, which ended with his sudden death from a heart attack when I was nine.

Later in the afternoon, when we take a break from our work, I approach her at the table with coffee and donuts. "How did you know that about my grandfather?" I ask her.

"It was simple," she says. "I saw you as a little girl with a grandfather. It was as clear as if it were a picture on TV."

Eventually I developed my own version of that TV screen. Once it was in place, it did not seem at all mysterious; it was very natural. As someone talked about her childhood, I could see the pictures she gave me, and could intuit the scenes she did not describe. (I always checked out my images to make certain they were accurate.)

This is an example of a special kind of intuitive/creative process. It is the opportunity to use moment-to-moment creativity in psychotherapy that kept the work exciting for me over so many years.

◆   ◆   ◆

A woman comes into my office for her second session. She seems to be in great distress. She puts her hand to her chest. She looks close to tears. "We all got into it last night," she says. "My kids, my husband…

She pauses.

"What happened?" I prompt.

Now her thoughts leap. "You know, there were eight kids in our family," she tells me, "and we were really poor."

At this moment, whatever I do is a creative choice. I have several options and my decision must be made in a split second.

Perhaps I will say nothing, and wait for her to continue her story. I may decide, at that moment, to table the childhood scene for later and ask her, now, for a fuller version of what happened in her own house last night. I might observe that her hand is against her chest and ask her what sensations she is experiencing just now. Or, I may use this opportunity to find out more about her childhood, gathering important background information we did not have time for in our first session.

There were eight kids in our family, and we were really poor. With that statement, I envision a room with a bare wood floor, children scrambling around, and a mother who is cooking, tired, pushing her hair up out of her eyes. It is like watching a movie. But I need more information.

"Where are you in the line up of eight?"

If she is the oldest, I imagine her helping with the younger kids; if she is in the middle, I suspect she did not get her full share of attention before the babies came along. If she is the baby she may have been raised mostly by an older sibling.

My inner movie continues. "Tell me about the house where you grew up." This gives both of us an opportunity to envision the same scene. I may, at another time, ask her to draw a floor plan of the house, and to tell me what feelings and memories she has as she mentally walks through each room.

How I respond at any moment is based on a mixture of experience and intuition, compassion and common sense. I always hold the larger context. I want the client to go deeper, learn something, take responsibility for her situation, feel empowered, expand her perspective, have a catharsis or come to some resolution. When my choice is good, one or more of these may happen. When my choice is misguided, I can always backtrack and steer her in another direction. I have learned to tell from my own inner antenna whether the direction I choose is helpful. If my intuition is accurate, I feel satisfaction as the work progresses. If my intuition is off, I feel uneasy. Each momentary awareness is part of the creative process.

◆　◆　◆

That process, for me, is not unlike writing this piece. I hold a larger context: describing the various ways that practicing psychotherapy provides opportunities for creativity. But as I write, I do not know exactly how that description will unfold. Each sentence emerges as a semi-surprise to me. At the end of writing a total piece, I am often astonished at how it turned out: it may be filled with examples I had no idea I would write. As I write, something moves aside and scenes appear, or images, or metaphors. As I write a poem, for instance, I may have the first line in my head before I find a pen, but the other lines emerge one by one. Only as I complete the line I am writing does the next line appear. It is a process that feels very easy when it is flowing, and seems impossible or mysterious at other times.

I think of creative process as an opportunity to express something that springs through me from an unknown place, that expresses something that is both me, and more-than-me. Some element comes through that is original, new, fresh or, hopefully, insightful. There is some way of thinking about a matter that puts it in a new light, turns it around so it can be seen from a new perspective, invites another person to share this perspective and then to add one of his own. It is an unfolding. It is a process that is dynamic rather than static: it moves, it takes on a life of its own; one dives into it and comes out the other side knowing a bit more, seeing a bit further, or with greater clarity.

Writing and doing psychotherapy have a common feeling for me. When the process is alive and well, I feel an ongoing sense of satisfaction, mixed with a slight amount of tension. There is intense concentration and focus. There is a sureness that the process will continue to flow, mixed with an equally strong feeling that this is hard work, like holding your breath under water; it might be easier to come up for air and go into the kitchen and find a carton of chocolate frozen yogurt. But I don't; I continue and, at the end, there is a feeling of immense well-being: not "look how good I am" satisfaction, but the joy of completion (even if it is not complete; even if the page has to be totally rewritten; even if the client is going to come in again next week with the problem still unresolved). There is a sense of *I did something that feels right, something that has not been done before, or has not been done in this way.* I feel I have reached a conclusion (for now) and I can relax inside and smile and feel good about it.

◆   ◆   ◆

Working with dreams, the creativity of client and therapist operates in tandem. The client tells me her dream. On my inner screen, I see a movie of what she is describing. She associates to her dream: what it reminds her of, where she thinks the images may have come from, what she thinks the dream is telling her. Often, however, she has no association. "I just don't get it at all," she tells me.

Meanwhile, I have some thoughts about the dream that come from my knowledge of her, of events in her life, and from my own ability to understand how symbols appear. Yet my interpretation of her symbols may be all wrong. I don't believe there is a universal meaning in every symbol, the way dream books often tell us. A train entering a tunnel may be a symbol of sexual intercourse in one person's dream, but in another it may be about a train trip she took as a child, or that she is going to take next month. Or it maybe a metaphor for a journey into the darkness, such as the therapy journey she is presently taking. In any case, the dream is a creation of the dreamer, a creative product of his or her unconscious mind. I can only guess, or help to decipher the code in the dream. If I am pointing in the right direction, the dreamer will pick up on it; if not, that little "click" of recognition will be absent. The decoding of the dream is a joint creative production between client and therapist. Even if I am sure, absolutely positive, about what that dream is saying, I need to present the thought in a way that allows room for him to accept or reject, or to discover it for himself.

◆   ◆   ◆

A creative therapist makes unlikely connective leaps of intuition. I was the recipient of such a gift, many years ago, in my first training group. I was trying to resolve what, for me, felt like a major problem, although no one else in the group empathized with me at all. My husband wanted to take me and the children on a trip to Hawaii during their spring break. I did not want to miss the training group sessions; I did not want to leave home; I wanted to stay where I was. My husband finally said, "If you don't go, we are going anyway." This was fair enough, but it left me very torn.

My co-trainees projected their own wishes for a vacation onto me and tried to convince me to change my mind. From their perspective, who would turn down a trip to Hawaii? This was very human, but not very helpful as therapy. Then our artful leader made a connective leap.

"Say this sentence," he instructed me. "*I want to belong.*"

As soon as I said the words I burst into tears. I knew he had discovered the real issue. It was not about missing meetings or being away from home. It was about having two passions: my new work and my family, and feeling forced to be left out of one or the other.

Once the issue of *belonging* was clear, somehow it did not seem so terrible to go on the trip. The group would still be there when I returned. What intrigued me, however, was how our leader got me to that place. None of the 25 therapists in the room, including me, had recognized that core issue. And if I had not burst into tears, which told me his intervention hit the right chord, I would still have been fussing about peripheral matters.

I asked him, once I had come up for air, "How did you know that was the issue?"

"It was just there," he said. "The sentence came into my head and I knew it fit."

That is creative intuition.

Sharing the Journey

The therapist must be willing to accompany the client as far, as deeply, as the client is willing to travel. To be able to do that without fear, the therapist must have taken a similar journey. If the client is traveling to China, it is not necessary that the therapist have been to that same continent, but she must be familiar with the exigencies of travel: missed connections, getting lost, not speaking the language.

Long ago, a very young woman came to see me. She began to tell me about her unhappiness with her family. They were from another culture, and imposed rules on her, such as not being able to go out on dates, that did not fit with the behavior of the young woman's American friends. "But," she said, "*you* can't possibly understand. You didn't grow up in a house with parents from the old world. And you probably don't even remember what it was like to be my age."

It was clear to me that she had never felt understood by her parents, and had difficulty trusting that understanding was possible, especially by someone a generation ahead of hers. But that is not why I am telling this story. The point I want to make is that she erroneously believed, as do many people, that unless you have experienced the exact circumstances, you cannot guide someone out of her dilemma.

Taken to the extreme, this would make finding a therapist extremely difficult. The depressive could only go to a therapist who had suffered from depression; the schizophrenic must find a therapist who also had that illness; the woman who was raped must find a therapist who also had been raped, a Catholic could only go to a Catholic therapist, and so forth. For the therapist, this approach certainly would limit one's practice to a ridiculous degree. It would also require inappropriate disclosure of one's private life before therapy even began.

Yet, there is a grain of truth here. Having experienced and overcome a situation does make the therapist more able to guide the client out of the forest. The problem is the confusion between plot and emotional understanding. By "plot" I mean the facts of one's story. The facts differ for every human being. But the emotional understanding is universal. The therapist who has explored the deeper dimensions of her own life will find the same dimensions of fear, grief, rage, difficult relationships and addictive behaviors that her clients bring in. They do not have to come from the same story to enable her to guide others.

It is not the giving of advice that is the essence of therapeutic change. It is the ability to facilitate the client's exploration into her own deeper self, her own experience, her own darkness. It is the difference between giving a lecture on how to scuba dive, or accompanying the novice as he puts on his scuba gear and descending with him to the underworld. It is the willingness to share the journey.

In imagination, I have accompanied frightened children down dark staircases to unlit basements where unspeakable things happened to them. I have run with them across fields and empty lots pursued by a large man, a stranger. I have, figuratively, held a child's hand as he climbed to the attic floor of a grandparent's house, lured by the promise of toys, and pushed open the heavy door to a room filled with cobwebs and guns. I have been in bedrooms with girls and their fathers, or grandfathers, or older brothers, or uncles, or their brother's friends, or their friend's fathers...I have watched attempted bathtub drownings by crazed mothers...have seen youngsters stagger home after being raped, only to be called liar, or slut, and beaten again by an enraged or drunk parent...

These are the secrets too terrible to tell. They emerge in small pieces. They may appear like flashes on a movie screen, or pain in the parts of the body that were injured, or internal voices shouting. The work of therapy is not only to help the client to remember what happened. The therapist must also guide her to feel what was felt then (the emotional work), and to recognize what beliefs came from the horrible experience (*I am bad* is a common one; also *the world is dangerous; I can't trust anyone*). Even that is not the end of the work. All her life, up to this point, the client has been re-experiencing the original feelings. They may manifest as amorphous despair and/or a wish to die. She has applied her original beliefs to every new situation that has come up in her life. Often this has occurred with no conscious memory of the original trauma. The therapist now has the job of validating the origins of the feelings and beliefs, while helping the client to separate the past from the present. The client must learn that there are safe places in the world, that there are people who can be trusted, that what happened was not her fault and she is not a bad person, that she is a survivor, not a victim.

These three phases: the memory of a traumatic event, the identification of feelings and beliefs about that event, and the corrective work of separating the present from the past, may occur consecutively, or simultaneously. In an ideal scenario (or a movie script) the client recalls the buried memory, immediately experiences and expresses the emotion, and then has a flash of insight, such as, "Oh! I see now that just because my father (abandoned/abused) me, I don't have to set it up so that every man I meet does the same thing." Therapy is seldom this ideal, however. Understanding comes in bits and pieces, and takes many repetitions before true change happens.

Sometimes a client may understand perfectly well at an intellectual level, but until she can experience the depth of her own pain, anger, sorrow and sense of betrayal, she will not be able to let go of her maladaptive patterns in the present. She may need to rage and weep. The therapist needs to support her through this process, which can take weeks, months, or years. The time depends on many factors: the extent of the original trauma, how much is buried, the willingness of the client to take risks in therapy, and the skill of the therapist, among others.

I have seen some clients become addicted to the release of long held pain: they do not believe they are "doing therapy right" unless a session is filled with sobbing. The release, which they were denied in childhood, feels like "coming home" to self. But the addiction to the pain/release cycle stops them from moving forward in the world. Here is a sensitive job for the therapist, who has spent a long time encouraging the client to take that journey into the darkness. Now it may seem as if the therapist is saying, "Okay, that's enough!" Then the therapist becomes the Bad Parent, perceived as giving permission to feel and then taking it away.

I tried to handle this dilemma by raising it for discussion at the beginning of a session, rather than during or after the release of emotion, when the person is most vulnerable and most apt to feel criticized. My approach was to keep a clear focus on moving forward in one's present life. Feeling the pain is a means to that goal, but not the goal in itself. For instance, if the client's goal is to have a healthy relationship in the present, it is useful to spend time focusing on the next healthy step in the relationship at hand. After the pain of the past has been explored and released, there is a time to let it go and focus on living more fully in the present. Finding the right balance between trips into the darkness and reemergence into the light is an aspect of the art and skill of the therapist.

The therapist also has the job of regulating timing. Too much material coming up too quickly can be dangerous. If the therapist senses too much emotional flooding happening in a session, she can bring the client back to the surface, and give the suggestion that no more need emerge during the week. She can also suggest activities that will keep the client grounded in the present, such as walking, exercising, cooking and tending to the children.

The opposite and more common corollary to emotional flooding is continued resistance to any painful material coming up at all. Kept buried underground, the blocked memories can fester and become poisonous. Yet, if the content that is emerging is too painful for the therapist to bear, he may become an unwitting accomplice in blocking the memories, somehow changing the subject or making "soothing" statements at the wrong moments. This is why it is important that the therapist have completed his own journey before becoming a guide into the dark for someone else.

In doing deep process work in therapy, it is best to leave some time at the end of the session to talk about what happened and how the client feels about the session itself. For a client going through the journey into the darkness, it is as necessary to learn how to surface as it is to learn how to dive. There needs to be support in the present in order to re-experience the pain of the past. The therapist provides some of that support, but also must help the client identify people in her life who can provide nurture and comfort.

The key to going through painful therapeutic work is *balance:* between darkness and light, pain and pleasure, past and present. Therapist and client share the responsibility: the therapist to help the client identify how to find balance, and the client to carry it out. When done in this manner, deep psychotherapeutic work can lead to depth and richness in life.

When the Work Flows

I sit quietly, both feet on the floor. My breathing is easy. I am relaxed and atten-tive. My mind has a single focus. I feel in harmony with myself and my surround-ings. I feel connected, moment by moment, to the person sitting across from me. Sometimes I know what she is going to say next, before the words leave her mouth. I know immediately, intuitively, when to be silent and when to speak. As my mind sees the scene of the story she is presenting, I ask questions to help her expand the scene. The openness with which she receives my offering lets me know that it was the right thing, said at the right moment.

"Where are you right now, in your mind?"

"I'm upstairs in my house, when I was little."

"How old are you?"

"I'm five. And I'm so scared. He's always around a corner, behind a door."

"Where are you exactly right now?

"I'm in bed. I'm under the covers. The covers are over my head. But still hear him."

A long silence.

"What is happening now?"

"He comes in and starts to pull down the covers, but now my mother is calling him and he goes away. I can't remember any more. It's all black now."

She is pale, hugging the white teddy bear I keep on the couch.

"Send your adult self in to comfort the little five year old."

Another silence, then a deep breath and a small smile. "I went in and held her and told her she is safe now, that I'll keep her safe, and that she didn't do any-thing wrong." She looks startled as she spoke. "I never realized that before. I always feel I've done something bad, even when I haven't."

Silence. I see her brow furrow; she is working something out. I stay with her in close attention, not moving, giving her space.

"I just heard him tell me not to tell Mommy what we did or I'll be in big trou-ble. And I don't know what he means because I didn't do anything but I'm scared of him. I never say anything." Silence. "Oh, God, I think he came in a lot and didn't leave...got in my bed...*no, don't touch me there, it hurts...*

She is back in my office now. I am still with her, in full attention. "Comfort her again," I say. I watch as she rocks the teddy bear. Her face relaxes. Another silence. Then she says "I told her I will always take care of her and she hugged me and fell asleep."

"That's good," I tell her softly. "You can do that for her any time, especially at night before you go to sleep, and in the morning when you are just waking up."

The session is nearly over. "I feel drained," she tells me.

"That's understandable. Just be very gentle with yourself the rest of today, and this week. Be good to yourself."

After she leaves, I am shaken. Yet I also feel a sense of warmth and satisfaction. The work was deep and flowed well. She was focused; I was facilitating, gently guiding, witnessing. She remembered a piece of her life that has affected her entire adulthood. I know that it will take time before she puts all the pieces together, but right now I am not concerned about that. Her voyage is launched. My job will be to help her regulate the timing, not to jump ship, and not to become flooded with too much, too soon. Her immediate goal must be to continue living her present life while uncovering and integrating these pieces of past trauma that have robbed her of safety, trust and pleasure. Then there will be a chance of learning to incorporate those qualities into her present life.

In fact, she has just taken a step toward the experiencing of safety and trust, here in my presence. I feel good about that, about offering the opportunity for that experience and having the offer accepted. That did not come about through long speeches, or arguing the point. It happened, I believe, at a level that is as much pre-verbal as verbal. It happened when my attention was stilled, my energy expanded, my state of consciousness altered, my vibrational level heightened, as happens in a deep meditation. In this state, she and I experience, non-verbally, an interconnectedness of being that enables her to drop inner barriers and move to that place in her own consciousness that needs to come forward next.

To work at this level is rewarding and even energizing for me. It can feel effortless, like taking one step and then the next, without worrying about how your foot will move or where it will land. When it happens, the sense is of wholeness, or completion. It is the deepest gift of this work we call psychotherapy. It is a two-way gift: I receive as much as I give. It is the deepest way to share our humanness.

Moving toward Wholeness

I am working with a new client. She is in my office for her second session. At this point, I have information about her current life, her family of origin, and the issues that brought her to my office (in this case, depression, an inability to maintain friendships, and job dissatisfaction). I also have my own impressions of her: she is attractive, has a quick mind, and has shown me photos of her paintings, which I am drawn to for their color and unique style, although I am not in any way an expert in this field.

This woman, like every client I work with, presents as a jigsaw puzzle with pieces yet to be uncovered and put into place. Pieces of the puzzle already exist, in plain view. Others are hidden: some from both of us, some from me, and some from the client herself. My job is to help her uncover, identify and own those pieces. Some pieces, very dark, need to be modified to make her life better. Others are beautiful as they are, but unseen or unacknowledged by her. The pieces that neither of us sees in this third session will come into clearer view as we proceed in the weeks and months that follow.

It is my job as therapist to see the dim outlines of the puzzle pieces when she cannot and to help her fill them in, fit them in place. It is her job as client to reveal to me, and to herself, what only she can know. Together we work to complete the jigsaw.

In order to complete it in a way that is healthy and beneficial, I carry a vision of the completed puzzle. This is what is termed, in humanistic psychology, "seeing the whole person." I see not only her pathology, her problems, her unhappiness; I also have a vision of her talent, her capacity for love, her fullest humanity. I see her as an infant, young child and teenager in her family, and sense who she might have been had the adults around her known how to nurture properly. I see her life as it was, as it is and, simultaneously, as it could become. I see her in her wholeness.

From this perspective, I am able to work with her to recognize her strengths as well as to change her dysfunctional behaviors. I envision this process as working with the soul that has been part of her since birth, but which met so many roadblocks along the way that it curled up in a corner to protect itself. Together we set out to clear away the roadblocks.

My vision of her wholeness is based upon human qualities I recognize in her which she may under-use or not see at all. I am very careful about how and when I share my vision with her: if I am premature it will likely be rejected by her. Instead, I try to guide her, very early in our work, toward an expression of how she would like her life, or even a single behavior, to change. If she can create her own vision, she has something positive to move toward. For many clients, this is a novel and startling idea. All they have known or allowed in their worlds has been the negative side. They have yet to learn that there is another way. If all I see is her pathology, I am not assisting her in moving elsewhere.

In the late 1950's, when Humanistic Psychology was first evolving, the idea behind the movement was to be an influence in psychology and psychotherapy that viewed patients as more than a bundle of pathologies (as Psychoanalysis did) and more than a bundle of conditioned behaviors (as Behaviorism did). The founders of humanistic psychology wanted to enlarge upon these ideas. They believed fervently that each person is unique and has a whole self, even though some of that wholeness has been blocked off. Each person has a life that is richest when he or she creates meaning and purpose; each person has an unfulfilled potential. Moving toward that is one's life path. Choice is always an option, even if one is trapped in the worst situation imaginable. (Viktor Frankl, in *Man's Search for Meaning*, writes of being a prisoner in a line marching toward the gas chambers in Europe and knowing he has a choice to stay in line or try to run away.)

Transpersonal psychology, which grew out of the humanistic perspective and goes a few steps farther, posits the existence of a soul, the ability to sense multi-dimensional layers of reality, and the necessity of nurturing the spiritual essence as an intrinsic part of the evolution of our human nature, and apart from any particular religion.

The three major schools of psychological theory and practice (analytic, behavioral and humanistic) are by no means mutually exclusive. Today, many therapists trained in psychoanalytic psychotherapy or behavioral therapy also incorporate humanistic values and perspectives. As a humanistic psychologist, I often use analytic theory to help me understand my clients. I also work with behavioral change when I sense that it is called for. But I find it crucial to look beyond pathology and behavioral patterns, to honor the human being who sits before me in her potential fullness and to teach her to honor herself.

We may never, my client and I, fill in every piece of the puzzle. Much of her growth may continue for years after she has left formal therapy. But I believe, from my experience, that my faith in the larger picture (the completed puzzle, her fullest human potential) is continually transmitted to her, both non-verbally and, when the time is ripe, in words. It is this quality of relationship, which humanistic psychologist Carl Rogers called "unconditional positive regard," that makes the difference in nurturing the self-esteem that can enable her to change her dysfunctional learned behaviors to ways that serve her better and to become a fuller human being.

The Bag of Tricks

Over the years I attended many training programs, weekend seminars and all-day lectures, in addition to my doctoral training, all designed to make me a better therapist by learning new theories and new techniques to implement those theories.

In Transactional Analysis (TA) training, I learned how to clarify issues by drawing diagrams. In Gestalt groups, I learned how to have the client pretend her mother was in the empty chair, and talk to her directly. Bioenergetic work taught me how to work with breathing, grounding and emotional release. Seminars on Ericksonian hypnosis taught me how to utilize metaphor and guided imagery. Cognitive therapy provided me with charts and homework for the client. Jungian therapy provided a useful approach to working with dreams. Family therapy suggested I invite in all the family members, including the grandparents and the dog.

Each school believed they had the best approach. After every training session, I emerged enthusiastic, eager to try out the new methodology on my unsuspecting clients. I was certain that this time I would help John or Maude get to the root of the problem, scream out the core issue, or suddenly have everything become clear using paper and pencil. At last, I would think, we can break through the barriers.

Wrong.

"I feel silly talking to an empty chair," they would tell me. Or, "You want me to do *what?*" when I suggested they lie down on a floor mat and kick, as we had done in Bioenergetic training. Or, "You know I never did my homework in school. I'll never go home now and make a list like that." Or, "Dreams? I never have any." Or, "My whole family? Are you kidding? My husband doesn't even know I'm coming here. He doesn't believe in therapy."

How come none of the people who did these methods so willingly in all the training videos we saw, ever found their way to *my* office?

I went back to what I had always done effectively: listening. Many of the people who came to see me had never learned to open up, in depth, to themselves or to another person. Their conversations with others were most often at a superficial, social level, even when they were talking about their problems. My listening, questioning, interest and empathy led the way for them to open, deepen, and trust.

Eventually, over time, I learned how to introduce one technique from my "bag of tricks" very gently, matching the specific method to the now-ready client. Done at the right time, it no longer felt to the client like an externally imposed assignment, but a useful experiment to serve his own purpose of going deeper and emerging with more inner freedom. The concept of "experiment" was important. It gave the control to the client. If the experience proved fruitful, she was willing to repeat it. If not, we could let it go. It was not right for her, at this time. No judgment was made on either of us. It was not a failure; it was simply a non-productive experience. We could try something else.

Most often, though, the techniques mentioned above, as well as others, were very powerful. That, of course, is the reason people hold back. There is a time when someone is ready for a powerful experience that will move her to a larger sphere, and a time when she is too frightened to attempt it. It is the art of the therapist to know when to honor the resistance, and when to give a gentle nudge to the part of the client who is truly ready to take a leap.

Listening

Listening as a therapist is different from ordinary listening. In ordinary listening, I may be doing several things at once: having a conversation on the kitchen phone while cutting up vegetables for a salad; tuning into a lecture on tape while driving the car in heavy traffic; talking to one of my grandchildren while trying to straighten up the living room. I hear what is being said, but not with my full concentration. My attention is divided.

In the therapy room, my listening is very focused. I do not have music playing. I turn off the ringer of the phone and let the answering machine take over. I do not move around looking for files or a pen. I become totally immersed in the words, the tone of voice, the pacing and cadence of speech, as well as the message of the person sitting across from me. If she is describing a scene from her life, I am in that scene as if I were reading a novel or watching a movie. I call this "deep listening."

Deep listening is a form of meditation. My consciousness is altered from everyday levels. I am in a state similar to a light trance, and my concentration is very intense. I slide into this state easily and may not recognize the shift until something unexpected, like a loud knock on the door, triggers a startle-reaction.

When the therapist is engaged in deep listening, the client, in a sort of "sympathetic resonance," may also enter a more focused state of consciousness. That is when the session becomes productive. At this deeper level there is more insight and more ability to change one's perspective and attitudes. Change becomes organic rather than a behavioral exercise.

There are other ways in which deep listening in a therapy session differs from ordinary listening. I am not only listening to the "plot" of the story, but to the phrases that indicate the attitude of the speaker toward the events she is relating. I am listening to hear the concealed emotions beneath her words; to understand what meaning the event has for her; to detect distortions in her view of a situation. I am also observing her facial expression and body language for cues to what is not being expressed verbally.

As I listen, I have to make moment to moment decisions. Do I remain silent or do I intervene? If I speak, do I make a statement (an interpretation) or do I ask a question? How do I phrase my words so that they are helpful rather than critical? What tone of voice do I need to use to be most effective in this moment, with this person?

It is not quite as difficult as it sounds on paper. Most of these decisions become intuitive and happen automatically. If I know the client even fairly well, I have already learned what is effective and what to avoid. If the client is new, there is more trial and error. Errors can always be corrected. They are not fatal, in most cases.

Each school of therapy, and each therapist, has a different style of listening. Some systems, like psychoanalysis, involve a quiet, uninterrupted listening, allowing the client to reach wherever he is going by whatever circuitous means. Others are much more directive, with a response for every few words the client utters. My own listening style is somewhat eclectic, and depends on my perception of my client's need.

As a child, I spent many hours listening to my father tell stories. If I tried to interrupt him (in fact, if anyone did) he raised his right hand, palm out, to indicate "Wait: let me finish." For me, that hand gesture was like a stop sign. Many years before I learned to drive, I learned to respond to that stop sign. It was conditioned into my very bones.

Over the years of being a therapist, I had two or three clients who were like my father: they told long stories, and held up the hand if I made any utterance at all before they were completely finished. With these people I could use my listening skills, but I was quite unable to recondition myself, while in the trance state of listening, to make any therapeutic interventions. Even if I did succeed in getting out an entire sentence while the hand was up, they would not listen to it, and were only irritated by my interruption. I do not list these sessions among my therapeutic successes. I was certainly entertained by some good story tellers, however.

There were other moments when my listening was not so ideal, such as toward the end of a long day. I would hear sentences in my own head that were saying, "Only 45 minutes and I can go to meet Bob for dinner." Or "It looks like a heavy snowstorm out there; I hope it won't be dangerous to drive home." I still looked to the client as if I were listening, and I was, but it was not from the same level of depth as at other times.

Beginning meditators often complain that they cannot "clear the mind" of the unwanted thoughts that run all over the place. Their teachers tell them to simply notice the thoughts, they are normal, not to expect them to never be present. The same is true of therapeutic listening. The thoughts in my head were an inner movie of my own. A story about the dying process of a client's mother brought images to my mind of my own mother's death; a story about a son in high school took me back 20 years to seeing my own sons at that age. It was like watching a split screen on the computer: the major part was the story of the client, and a small square in the lower corner was a simultaneous, but not totally intrusive, film of my own life. They played in parallel.

With experience, I learned how to utilize my inner film to be therapeutically helpful. Knowing how I felt, I sensed how my clients might feel. I could anticipate what they would tell me. At the clearest moments, I began to hear what the client was about to say just before she said it. I would be thinking, "She is telling me about her father, but where was her mother?" and she would say, "My mother was…" Or, a client would say, "I have to tell you something I haven't talked about before." I would have a flash picture of a child in bed at night in terror, and she would say, "My father used to come into my room…" This is not an example of being "psychic." It is a description of what happens when the level of listening is finely attuned. Maybe that is the same thing under a different name. But it is not "paranormal" and it is not unusual. It happens for good listeners all the time.

Sometimes listening is enough. The therapist does not need any brilliant questions or fancy techniques. Just to be able to tell one's story to a non-judgmental, interested, accepting other can be, in itself, therapeutic. Now the client no longer holds a heavy secret all by herself. The burden is lightened. The guilt carried from childhood may begin to dissolve. She realizes, just through telling the story out loud for the first time, that what happened was not the fault of a seven year old child. She hears her own story from an adult perspective. She stops feeling that she is "bad."

This is the "best case" scenario. More often it takes many sessions, many tellings, many repetitions, to work out all the areas where guilt and self-blame lie undetected, or to recall the details. There maybe the need to come to grips with not only what happened, but with the loss of an idealized illusion about a parent or other significant figure from childhood. The therapist must be willing to listen again and again, each time, pointing up another small particle of matter that has lain on the floor undetected, for many years.

When my listening is deep and uninterrupted, my sense of time may be distorted. The 50 minute session may seem very brief, and there is a tendency to run over the allotted time. On the other hand, just as in meditation, some inner knowing tells me to the minute exactly what time it is. Just to be sure, I keep my portable clock where I can easily glance at the time.

Deep listening differs from ordinary listening in the way that scuba diving differs from swimming. When you scuba dive in the ocean, the fish and corral that are hidden from a swimmer's view become vivid, three dimensional realities. Staying on the surface may feel safer and more familiar, but the experience is more meaningful when you see what is below. If the therapist leads the way, it is likely the client will follow.

Sleepiness

Sometimes, while concentrating deeply, I would become very sleepy. This happened mostly at the end of the afternoon, about 4:00 p.m. I always felt sorry for my four o'clock clients. Once I was stifling a yawn, and the woman who was with me said, "Oh, I'm sorry, I must be really boring." She had believed that was true all her life, and my yawn fit right in to her distorted pattern.

I tried to explain that at a certain hour of the day my body chemistry shifted and the yawn had nothing to do with her and she was not boring. We explored why she thought she was boring, even when someone was not yawning. But it was too late. I imagine that to this day she holds the image of pouring out her deepest pain to a psychologist who yawned.

It happened another time, when I was not breathing very deeply and suddenly just had to take a deep breath. It was so deep that it looked and felt like a yawn. This time the man across from me said, "I guess you didn't get enough sleep last night." He was one who stayed up until 3:00 or 4:00 in the morning himself. So we talked a bit about the nature of projection and how he was attributing to me a behavior that belonged to him. Again, I tried to explain that I am a shallow breather and every so often my body compensates with a huge breath that looks like a yawn. He wasn't buying it. "You must have been out partying too late," he said. "Does your husband know where you were?"

We talked about how he liked to deflect the conversation from himself when the material became uncomfortable, but it didn't work. I think that, deep down, he, too, thought he was boring me. He quit therapy a session or two later.

When I felt the urge to yawn, I tried to inhale with my mouth closed so that I would not look like I was yawning. Try it—it's not easy. Your throat muscles extend and you really don't fool anyone. And it is only partially satisfying; the urge to yawn simply repeats itself.

Sometimes I tried a defensive maneuver. At the start of the session, I would say, "I have a problem with yawning at this time of day. I want you to know that beforehand, because it has to do with my physiological patterns, and not with you or anything you may be talking about."

Sometimes this was accepted, but some clients simply peered at me anxiously from behind their words, trying to anticipate when they were going to lose their therapist to sleep.

Besides yawning, there was the problem of overwhelming sleepiness. It helped to have a client who would go deeply into a past memory with her eyes closed for better concentration. Then, if I had to close my eyes for a brief second, or if they closed of their own accord, she couldn't tell. But there was always the worry: *what if she opens her eyes and sees that mine are shut?* I never went to sleep in the sense of not listening to what was being said. But sometimes the urge to shut my eyes was irresistible. It reminded me of the way I felt in college during a lecture, when I had just come from three other lectures. In those classes I tried to sit near the back, so the professor would not see me falling asleep right in his face.

So there we were in my office, me and someone who was paying me a lot of money to listen, cure, and make her feel better. And I was fighting sleepiness. What to do? I moved around in my chair a lot. I crossed my legs, uncrossed them, crossed them in the other direction. Shifted my body from slouched to upright. Moved the position of my arms. Propped my eyelids open as if with two sticks. Inhaled deeply without letting it turn into a yawn. Sometimes it helped, for a few minutes.

Sessions when I was asked by the client to use relaxation or hypnotic trance presented another issue. During trance induction, the hypnotist often "goes under" with the client. Actually, this synchronicity of mental states makes hypnosis more effective. During an induction I often felt my words coming more and more slowly—not only because that was the best technique, which it is, but because I myself was going so deep that I *couldn't* speak any faster. Sometimes there was a long pause between the first half of my sentence and the second half, during which time the client also fell into deep trance. Then I would rouse myself and do my work, suggesting metaphors or asking questions that helped her accomplish whatever was our agreed upon task. Trance was another time when I could safely close my eyes, since hers were also closed, and indulge in 30 seconds of total rest, waking myself up at the end of that brief time with the suggestion *as I open my eyes I feel wide awake and alert.* This is self-hypnosis, and, for any reader who wants to try it, it does work.

Even in my sleepiest moments, it was always eyes closed but peeking: making sure that I was aware of my client and her moment to moment process—and that she would not catch me with my lids down, so to speak. For the most part, however, I spent the majority of time in my chosen profession fully awake. And I was almost never bored.

PART IV

Pitfalls, Problems and Puzzles

My Mother's Rules

.

When I was quite young, my mother taught me sensible rules for living in the world with kindness. At least three of these rules were relevant to my later career as a psychotherapist: one helpful, two definitely not so helpful.

My mother taught me, very young, to keep secrets. When I was ten, she overheard me telling Suzanne something Pearl had confided in me about her parents. My mother was very upset with me. Later, while she was cooking dinner and I was setting the table, she tried not to sound angry. "Never tell one friend what another told you in confidence," she said, "or you'll lose both of them. The one you tell will know you can't be trusted, and the one you betrayed will eventually find out."

I never asked my mother how she knew things like that; it never occurred to me to question her wisdom. She was Mother. She knew. By the time I was in my teens, and dating boys, I had learned not only to keep the secrets of others, but my own. This, plus the fact that I seldom gossiped, annoyed my girlfriends, who loved to tell everything to anyone who would listen, but felt cheated when I wouldn't do the same.

All of this was excellent training for being a psychotherapist. I never had any difficulty honoring the code of ethics regarding confidentiality. If anything, I leaned the other way. I had difficulty making case presentations in group supervision without feeling guilt about betraying a client. At conferences, when cases were presented by speakers, or worse, when they showed videotaped sessions, I felt extremely uncomfortable, as if I were forced to be a voyeur. And I am appalled when I hear my colleagues tell stories about their patients at social gatherings, even when they don't use names.

Keeping secrets is, after all, one of the basic tenets of psychotherapy. It has to do with the issue of trust. A client must be able to trust that what she tells her therapist will not be repeated. For a great many people in our society, trust is a difficult issue, in general. So it is imperative that the client be able, in reality, to trust the therapist. In this way she can learn that it is possible to trust others in her life. The client is telling stories that not only have been secrets from others in her life, but often, hidden from her own awareness. In a sense, she has secrets from herself. It can be excruciatingly difficult to stumble over such information unexpectedly. If it has been suppressed, it is because the nature of the information was intrinsically too disturbing to carry in consciousness.

How important, then, to be able to tell someone and to know that the secret will go no farther than the walls of the room, unless the client herself decides to tell someone. It is, after all, her secret to keep—or to share.

Keeping secrets (or, in the jargon of the profession, maintaining confidentiality) is not always a simple matter. Problems can arise when partners in a relationship want the therapist to collude in keeping secrets from the spouse. A similar situation occurs when the therapist is working with a child and his parents. If the child trusts the therapist enough to reveal important information that Mom or Dad don't know about, telling the parents without his acquiescence could destroy his trust in others for many years, if not for life. But Mom and Dad are paying for these sessions. What happens when they find out the therapist was not leveling with them?

A safeguard for the therapist and for the good of the treatment involves having clarity right from the beginning. The child needs to know that any information that could lead to harm for him or for others must be shared with Mom and Dad. The parents need to know that their child has a right to some privacy, and leave it to the professional discretion of the therapist to protect their child's secrets.

There are times in therapy when it is unethical and sometimes illegal to keep secrets. If a client threatens to harm himself or another person, the law in many states (one of these being Michigan, where I live) requires that the family be told or the person under threat be alerted that he or she is in danger. Failure to take this preventative action can result in a lawsuit against the therapist if the client acts on his threats. Also, if the therapist suspects that a child in his treatment is being abused or otherwise endangered, it is legally required that the therapist report this to the proper investigative authorities.

A woman comes to see me. "You were my older sister's therapist last year," she tells me. "I saw all the wonderful changes she made in her life, and I want you to help me, too."

Seemingly, there is no problem here. The first woman has terminated therapy, and has referred the second one to me. I must lock out of my mind, however, any secrets I might already hold that involve this new client. I take care of privacy issues in the first session, by making it very clear that anything she says to me is totally confidential and making sure she understands that anything I know about her sister is also a sealed book. In fact, over time, as I keep that first confidentiality, it is evidence to her that I can be trusted with her secrets, too.

At times I have had sessions with women whose adult daughters have contacted me to work out issues with their mothers. In most cases, I recommend that we have a session in which both are present, and I facilitate their conversation with each other, much as I might do in a marital session. On occasion, I have agreed, with the blessings of the mother, to see the daughter alone for one or two sessions. If the daughter needs further help, I refer her to someone else. I had to learn to do that the hard way. I found that, because of confidentiality issues, I was just asking for trouble if I continued to see both of them individually.

Mostly, I avoided the above problems by treating only unrelated clients. Of course, similar issues could arise when a client referred her friends or colleagues. Usually, however, this was less of a problem than with family members or partners who lived together because the relationship was less intertwined.

I found the issue of confidentiality could arise outside my office, too. A friend of mine might refer a relative of hers. Two months later she could ask me, "How is my cousin doing in therapy?" That is a double bind question, like, "When did you stop beating your wife?" The ethics of confidentiality require that I not even reveal if someone is in (or still in) treatment with me. So I have to say to my friend, the good referral source, "I really can't discuss anything about him, including whether or not he is in therapy." That doesn't rate points on the friendship scale, but it is direct and ethical. I can also suggest that she ask him directly. Clients are free to talk about any aspect of their therapy, including what they think of the therapist.

Most of the time, in most sessions, I said very little about my own life. On occasion, however, I found it useful to briefly reveal some story of my own when it had direct bearing on letting the client know that I understood, not only as a professional, but as another human being. In those rare situations, I reminded the client of our confidentiality contract, and requested that she honor it toward my sharing, as I did toward hers.

Another aspect of confidentiality arises regarding insurance carriers who want to know what they are paying for, and why. I guess I can't blame them for asking. I am very concerned, however, about revelations that could be potentially damaging in the wrong hands, especially if the insurance is handled through the corporation where the client works. For example, I never wrote in my notes, or on insurance company forms, if a client was lesbian or gay or undecided as to sexual orientation. I only noted: "has relationship issues." I used the word "friend" in my notes, instead of "lover," and avoided pronouns such as "he" or "she." I also, as stated earlier, avoided the use of certain diagnostic labels that could tag someone in a negative way.

My case notes were written in an abbreviated manner to remind myself of what I needed to remember, but which would be extremely vague if an outsider were to read them. My files were always in a locked cabinet. Today, post-retirement, thousands of secrets about hundreds of people over a span of a quarter-century are locked in the file cabinet of my brain. Some are vivid; others seem to be written in quickly-fading ink. They will never be shared.

◆   ◆   ◆

In addition to teaching me to keep secrets, my mother also taught me two rules which were useful in learning to be polite, but not helpful to me as a therapist. I had to revise them in order to do my work.

The first was: it is not polite to bring up the subject of people's obvious physical deformities or disabilities. "It embarrasses them," she told me. "Just save your questions and ask me later, when the person is not around."

This bit of good manners, acquired when I was five and pointed at a man with a wooden leg, was definitely not useful to me as a therapist. Like my mother's many morality lessons, I took it in young, heard it on many occasions (if not in regard to my own behavior, then perhaps that of younger children in the neighborhood) and believed it unquestioningly for all time.

Early in my career as a TA group leader, I had a client with noticeably deformed fingers. Every week I vowed to myself to ask her about that feature, but never could find the right words. The group ended, and I had never asked.

A year later, this client phoned asking to see me privately. I couldn't go home and ask my mother what to do (she had died, but her rules lived on) but I did ask my own therapist, who told me that it is common practice to take a good medical history. (Here was one disadvantage of doing one's career in reverse.)

Since we were now starting over, I was able to ask the client in a matter-of-fact way about childhood illnesses. It turned out that she had juvenile rheumatoid arthritis, and living with the pain had played a significant role in her psychological development. It would have been useful to have known that earlier.

◆   ◆   ◆

I was an obedient child, but I was also a quiet rebel. Perhaps that was why I did not have difficulty with mother's third dictum, "Don't ask personal questions." I had no problem breaking that rule. Other than asking about physical deformities, which I eventually learned to do in a professional manner, I found that I deeply appreciated the directness of asking personal question. That is, after all, the basic tool of all forms of therapy. The expectation of the profession strongly overruled what my mother had taught me in the interests of "good manners." I asked personal questions of everyone, all day, for years. Breaking that rule legitimately was a satisfying step in a successful career. I know that even my mother would agree.

Needing to Feel Needed

It's not news that clients need their therapists. That is transference. It is also reality: if there was no need, there would be no therapy.

But how about the other way around? How much do therapists need their clients? (This is called "counter-transference.")

My observation is: we need our clients more than we like to admit.

Being needed as an adult can give us a sense of purpose or meaning in life. But even more basic than that, being needed tells us we are noticed, that someone knows we exist. In childhood, this expresses itself as competition for who is most "popular."

When I was in elementary school, the kid who felt the most popular was the one who received the most valentines, or the one who was picked first for a baseball team, or the one who got invited to the most birthday parties. In high school, the girl who felt popular was the one asked out on dates by the most boys. For the boys, it was the one who "made out" with the most girls. (We're talking early 1950's here, kids, way before AIDS or the sexual revolution. "Making out" stopped far short of today's "hooking up.") Life could be a lot of fun…if you were popular.

We're talking about *numbers.*

There were many times when I thought this mentality had locked itself into the psyches of some of my colleagues. It had to do with self esteem, when we were school kids, and, unfortunately, it still seemed connected to that issue. "How many clients did you see today?" was the form it took in clinics where I worked. I, too, got caught into that mentality when I was new to the game.

At one clinic, there was a loose-leaf notebook into which all of us wrote down our appointments for the week. This was so that the secretaries, who scheduled room assignments, would know where to put people. I must confess that when I wrote down my 10 or 15 *weekly* appointments on my page, I snuck a look at the pages of the others. *Every line was filled!* Some were scheduling 12 people a *day,* "back to back," as it was called. Every 45 minutes, with no break between sessions. Of course, they had been in the profession many years and I was a newcomer. No matter.

I was the kid with two valentines while the others had a bagful.

The Adult in me wondered, "Don't they ever have to go to the bathroom? Do they eat lunch?" But the Kid felt like she was two grades behind.

Once, at that clinic, I overheard a (loud) conversation in the hallway between two other therapists. One was saying, "Remember when I told you I saw 38 people last week? Well, I forgot to add the 16 in my two groups, so I really saw 54. Isn't that amazing?"

She won the prize that week for Most Popular Girl in the class, no doubt about it.

Needing outside reassurance of worth by counting numbers is a dangerous trap for therapists. Unless you possess unlimited energy and powers of concentration, how well can you serve the folks who come in at the end of the day, when most human beings are winding down into tiredness? How many cases must you take on that are not in your area of skill, in order to have such high numbers? When I see therapists advertise that they specialize in "children, adolescents, adults, families, individuals and group therapy," I am a bit suspicious of their motivation. When I see a therapist interview an entire family, and than take on each member as an individual client, calling it "family therapy," I am again mistrustful. When a therapist (other than an analyst) tells all his clients "if you want to work with me, you must come three times a week" (or, "You must come twice a week and come to group therapy weekly, in addition") I am again wary.

There is, of course, a second obvious motive for all the above: more clients equal more money. But: I have seen therapists do all the above, and not have time to do the paperwork required by the insurance companies in order to get paid. Or not have time to do their own billing. Or not require their clients to pay weekly, thus building up huge bills that the client could not afford. Additionally, I have known therapists with huge caseloads who were owed many thousands of dollars by their clinic managers.

My conclusion is: huge caseloads are not always or only about money. They are also about feeling needed. Popular. Important. They have to do with ego-boosting.

No therapist will ever admit this, however.

An indication that this is so happens when caseloads fall. There is a very real fear, in any business, when the numbers fall: *Will clients/patients/customers return? Can I pay the rent? Can I feed my family?* The therapy business, like many others, is seasonal. Numbers drop in summer, when people go on vacations or feel better because of the weather; they drop again just before Christmas, when people are busy preparing and buying gifts; they are down just after Christmas, when people are paying off their debts, and then rise sharply because of the trauma and disappointments of the unfulfilled expectations at Christmas time. This happens like clockwork, every year. Yet every year, therapists get depressed because their numbers are down. They begin to question their own self-worth. They forget that it is the annual Christmas slump, and think maybe they should have gone into the family hardware business after all.

There are other ways that therapists reveal their need to feel needed. One way is the amount of time they spend on the telephone with clients while they (the therapists) are supposedly away on vacation, or off at a conference. Once, in the days before cell phones, I was at a seminar where a central hallway held one public telephone. Every time there was a break, one of the therapists could be heard talking to one of her clients, giving her advice on how to get through the rest of the day. I am not questioning whether the advice was good; it probably was. But it was the loud voice and public way that she engaged in these conversations that said to anyone who walked by, "Someone needs me; I have importance."

A dangerous way the therapist may keep her caseload high and continue to feel "popular" is to undermine the recognition of the client that he is, indeed, ready to terminate treatment. (To clients who maybe reading this, it must be stated that sometimes the client wants to quit when it is truly too early, before gains have been integrated, or to avoid painful material that is emerging.) When someone has achieved his goal in therapy, both he and the therapist know it. But if the therapist has unfulfilled and unrecognized needs to feel needed, liked or popular (as well as rich) by having as many clients as possible, she might tell the client that he is just not ready to leave. The key work here is "unrecognized." A therapist who is conscious of her own issues can make a choice to work them out elsewhere, and simply admit to her own sense of loss when a client is terminating. It is the unconscious therapist who is the danger here. (Note: the termination issue may be obsolete by the time you read this chapter, since now it is often third-party payers who decide who is ready to end therapy, usually based on finances rather than client need.)

A criticism of psychotherapy as a social institution, and a fear of most clients, is the issue of dependency. Clients come into therapy feeling needy, often with one foot out the door, protesting, "I don't want to become dependent on you. I don't want to use therapy as a crutch." The fear is well founded and the solution is that what therapy is really about is helping people to feel empowered and autonomous. It is, therefore, incumbent upon the professional in the therapeutic relationship to recognize his/her own dependency needs and not indulge them at the expense of the client.

Lest I sound too judgmental of my colleagues, I must confess that I recognize all of the above because I have been aware of each of these tendencies in myself at various times. Hopefully, I did not act on them. If this confession leaves me open to the charge that I am projecting my motivations onto others, so be it.

I recognized this need in myself in yet another behavior: my addiction to checking my office phone machine quite frequently, from wherever I may have been. When there were no calls, I felt a mixture of relief and disappointment. The relief was that I could continue uninterrupted with my activities away from the office. The disappointment was that no one needed me.

Why I Didn't Love Couples

It is 4:50 p.m. In ten minutes I have an appointment with a married couple, their second session. I rearrange the chairs in the office so that we can sit in a sort of triangle where we can all see one another without excessive head turning. I have found that when a couple sits side by side on my sofa, they are unable to look directly at one another to see facial expressions and other non-verbal communications.

I check my notes from the previous week. We had a satisfactory first session and I sent them home with a "homework" assignment designed to reset the temperature of their relationship from below freezing to a more tolerable climate. I am imagining that we will begin with a report of how that went, when I hear the door to the waiting room open. I expect to hear conversation between them. All is silent.

I go out to greet them but find that only the wife is there. "Oh, Dr. Goren," she says, "my husband will be about half an hour late. He just called my cell phone." She rises to enter my office. "But I'm kind of glad," she continues, "because I want to talk to you about something private before he comes in."

In my early years as a therapist I would have simply invited her in, eager to hear what she had to tell me. Now, older and wiser, I see red flags wave. I have learned through my earlier mistakes that if I see her alone, he will enter as an outsider and likely feel that we (two women) are aligned against him.

Further, if she tells me something that is a deep secret (here I panic: what if she wants to tell me she is having an affair?) I am placed in a double-bind. If I let him know, I am betraying her confidentiality. If I do not, I am colluding with her against him. Yet if I do not allow her to confide in me, I am working without full information. Also, she may decide to quit, since what good is a therapist who won't listen to you? I can ask her to remain in the waiting room until he comes in, which will assure her anger. (*She* has showed up, after all. It is not her fault he is late. They will be charged for the full session, but we will only have twenty minutes together, because I have another client scheduled at 6:00 p.m.)

I have only a split second to decide what to do.

In my various trainings, workshops, supervision sessions and book-learning, there were several basic principles I learned about working with couples. The first is to establish immediately that the therapist is the person in charge of the treatment. A second is to help the couple learn and practice good communication techniques—how to speak, how to listen—which they can use all the time, not only in my office. A third is to maintain balance: treating each member of the couple equally, and not being perceived as favoring one over the other. There were more, but these three were fairly universal. They made sense to me in the abstract. In practice, they were difficult to carry out. The husband in this case has just undermined all of them. By deciding not to be there, he is putting himself in charge of the process for today, eliminating the possibility of communicating at all, and sabotaging the issue of balance. The wife is doing the same thing. This situation is unlike individual therapy, where I want the client to share her secrets. If I follow this wife's agenda, I am abandoning my own authority and damaging the perception of balance.

My error was not to make the rules clear in the first session. For now, I usher her into my office to explain. "I have a policy about secrets," I tell her. "Information needs to be shared in session with both of you present."

She stares at me in disbelief. *A therapist who won't listen to your problem?* I imagine she is thinking. *What is this?*

"Look," I tell her, "you and your husband requested work as a couple. I have an equal obligation to both of you. If you ask me to keep a secret from him while we are working together, it puts me in a very difficult situation. I am a colluder with you. It is against my ethics to work that way."

What I couldn't tell her was that I had made the error of colluding many years earlier, and I have always regretted it. The wife was my individual client for years. I knew that she had been unfaithful and that he did not know. At some point I agreed, reluctantly, to do couple therapy with her and her husband. "He feels safe with you," she said. "He won't go to anyone else." I was seduced into agreeing. I saw them together, and later saw him alone. I kept her secret.

A year down the line, however, the husband dropped out of treatment with no warning. Later the wife phoned to tell me she had finally moved out. She told him that she had been having an affair, and when he asked if I had known about it, she said, *Yes.* I knew he must have felt betrayed by both his wife and by me, his therapist. I felt terrible. I vowed never to be in that spot again.

But I was about to be. "You can either share this information in his presence," I told her," or you can come to see me for individual therapy, and I will refer the two of you to a colleague for couple therapy."

Fortunately, her husband walked in just then. I filled in the policy information I had forgotten to discuss in the first session, including my rule that if they were to work as a couple, they must both be present. If that were not possible, they must cancel 24 hours in advance to avoid being charged. If one came alone, their work together was being jeopardized.

I hated having all these rules. I hated enforcing them. Yet I found that without them, the therapy got booby-trapped.

In another memorable session with a new couple, the wife came to the first (and only) appointment with a long list of written grievances. They were inscribed on both sides of a legal sized sheet of lined yellow paper, which she unfurled dramatically as soon as she and her husband sat down. With no further ado, she began to read aloud. Interrupting, I told her that we would get to her list in due time, but this was our first meeting, and there were some things we had to do first. It was not useful to begin this way.

The wife was furious that I was daring to run the session rather than letting her do it. (I suspect she had been rehearsing this reading for months.) Midway through our power struggle, she stood up dramatically and said, "My doctor recommended you. I'll see to it that he never sends anyone to you again." She collected her purse, her coat and her husband and stormed out without paying, her list still unread.

Women, I found, generally initiated the couple therapy, and their men followed, reluctantly. The woman often had an unspoken agenda of her own: that I would convince her husband that she was right. She came in with the assumption that I would be on her side in any conflict because she knew she was right and I, being a woman, would naturally see that. I continually had to explain that I was not an advocate, as an attorney might be, but a neutral party helping them to hear one another. Yet, whenever I asked the husband for his perspective, it was viewed by her as a betrayal. *(He's a non-person. Why do you want his opinion?)*

To facilitate couples in actually hearing what their partners were saying, I often used a common empathy-training technique of asking the listener to repeat back what they heard *before* responding to it. A simple example of this might be:

Wife: When you watch football all day and never talk to me, I feel like you don't care about me."
Therapist: Tell Mary what you are hearing her say.
Husband: (textbook response): You feel like the football game is more important to me than you are."

The textbook response always works—in the textbook. In real life the dialogue is more like this:

> **Wife**: When you watch football all day and never talk to me, I feel like you don't care about me.
> **Therapist**: Tell Mary what you heard her say.
> **Husband**: She thinks I'm a lazy slob who never does any work around the house, as if I don't work 60 hours a week and deserve a Sunday off.

Back to square one.

I never found much correlation between good therapy and improved relationships. I could carry on the best of sessions: the husband and wife were communicating effectively, listening, caring, faithfully doing their homework. Then, a year after a successful treatment and our agreed-on termination, they were engaged in the bitterest of divorces.

On the other hand, I recall my work with another couple when the sessions were a disaster. The tensions and anger were so intense that I had to open my windows to air out the office for the rest of the day. They didn't listen to anything I said. They just wanted to fight in my presence. Perhaps they got off on having an audience. Before I could kick them out of therapy, they fired me. The wife just stood up and left in the middle of a fight, without saying goodbye. The husband looked at me, shrugged, and followed soon after. I felt wiped out.

Three years later I received a Christmas card from them. The wife wrote, "You may not believe it, but our work with you was incredibly helpful. We are still married, have bought a new house, the children are doing well and we are very happy together. Thank you for putting up with us." The card was signed by both of them.

Despite this "success," for which I take no credit at all, I do not look back at work with couples as one of the highlights of my career. I have colleagues who love to work with couples. I referred many people to them. I don't know if they were any more successful than I was but they enjoyed it more. Maybe they had fewer rules.

Beginning therapists, do not let me discourage you. There are new books, new techniques and new rules. There are more than enough troubled couples to go around. You may love it.

Touching and Holding

Nothing has been more controversial in the field of psychotherapy than the issue of whether it is ever proper for the therapist to touch a client.

At one end of the field stand the psychodynamic/psychoanalytic therapists. Their answer is totally, unequivocally *No*. At the other end are the liberal/radical humanists, who feel it is sometimes inhuman to deny the touch of a hug. In the middle are the other hundreds of thousands of confused therapists who have received a mixture of training and don't know what to believe.

(This is not about having sex. All sides agree that it is immoral, unethical, illegal and just plain stupid to for a therapist to have sex with a client, although there are probably therapists on both sides of the issue who have done so. Any client who faces this dilemma should get out immediately and report the therapist to the local professional organization of which he/she is a member. If the client is attracted to the therapist and wants the sexual relationship, she should get out even faster.)

Non-sexual touch: that is controversial enough.

Here in brief is the background:

Freud, the Father of Psychoanalysis, where the entire field of psychotherapy began, was a genius at understanding the human psyche, but a bit uncomfortable in social relationships. His patients (they were not "clients" and still are "patients" to modern-day analysts) would lie on a couch and he would sit behind them where he could see them but they could not see him. He was not comfortable being stared at all day. Also, in the true spirit of the Victorian era in Europe, he did not believe in any sort of physical contact. Not even a handshake at the final session.

Freud's followers have built every one of his idiosyncrasies into a body of theory that has become as sacrosanct to the generations of his followers as any religion. There is no touch, and that's that.

Enter the other side: Freud died in the middle of the 20th century. The social climate changed. New therapies arose. Many of their founders were originally disciples of Freud, but split off, adding new theories to the work. Wilhelm Reich introduced the concept of analyzing not only the psyche, but the musculature system, where repressed feelings lurk. Alexander Lowen expanded Reich's work into a system he named Bioenergetics. Both Reich and Lowen worked directly with the body, as do their followers. Physical touch is often a necessary part of the work. When Eric Berne developed Transactional Analysis (TA) in the '60's, it did not involve more than a handshake. Then it was adopted by the humanistic psychology movement, and altered. The "human potential" movement, which grew out of humanistic psychology, was a huge promoter of groups in which hugging was as natural as saying "Good morning."

New theories and practices began to emerge like spring grass. One of them was called reparenting, and that is where much of the controversy began. When I was first taught reparenting, it was within the context of the TA world. A woman named Jacqueline Schiff, MSW, a TA therapist in California, had developed a radical treatment for young people who had been diagnosed as schizophrenic. She adopted them and made them part of her family, then allowed them to regress (to become like infants, then slowly grow up) and during the regression, taught them principals of being human which they had not learned in their families of origin. They learned such things as: *you are lovable, you are valuable, you are a worthwhile human being, this behavior is acceptable and that is not; I can love you unconditionally and still insist that you behave in an acceptable way,* and so forth.

The work of Jacqueline Schiff was highly controversial because it broke every rule of therapy, but it seemed to work. Many of these previously incurable, schizophrenic adolescents became healthy, upright citizens, and some even went on to become TA therapists, helping others who had been like them.

Reparenting, as it went on in Jackie's home, involved going right back to infancy, being allowed to cry, to eliminate into a diaper, to drink from a bottle, and to be held the way human infants need to be held in order to grow up healthy.

In the 70's, before all the data was in, it seemed that a miracle was in progress. Jackie traveled around the U.S. and gave training workshops to hundreds of eager therapists. Her 1970's book, *All my Children*, sold hundreds of thousands of copies. Other trainers taught her methods in their own workshops and training programs. Many therapists who learned reparenting techniques worked in outpatient clinics or did private therapy. They believed that reparenting could and should be adapted for their own settings. If their patients, or clients, had been deprived of human touch as infants, they could now have a corrective experience. The therapist and client would "contract" (agree) to spend a certain amount of each session with the client in a regressed state, (but not go so far, in an hour, as to include diapering) and the therapist would become the "good parent" and hold the "baby," who might be a 45 year old, who, in this regressed state, would take in to her (or his) psyche new messages about her core value.

This began in the newly free era of the late '60s and '70's. By the time I learned about reparenting, in the mid '70's, hundreds upon hundreds of therapists around the United States were using this technique. The traditionalists were appalled. The lines had been drawn.

Initially, I believed that reparenting made good sense, and I incorporated it into my work with some clients, especially in group settings. My own experience on the receiving end had been significant:

I was attending a weekend training marathon. About twenty-five of us, all therapists or therapists-in-training, sat on pillows in a large carpeted room that had a swimming pool at one end. Stan, our trainer, sat at the other end. Each of us, in turn, made a contract for the weekend involving something about ourselves that we wanted to change. I wanted to eliminate the irrationally strong anger that sprang up when I perceived someone as ignoring or downplaying my emotions.

"Get in touch with the feeling," Stan, asked of me. I recalled the last time I had experienced this (yesterday, before coming to the marathon). "How old are you?" he asked. Without a hesitation I said, "About one." I don't know how I knew that, but as soon as I said it, I knew the roots went back that far.

"Why don't you contract to be one year old for part of this weekend, and get reparented," Stan suggested. "Louise can be your mother." Louise was a helper at the weekend, a woman with grown children, a therapist, and a warm, nurturing woman. The suggestion to do this had two purposes: it was therapy for me, and also would give me an experiential knowledge of how reparenting could feel to a client.

Louise and I found a comfortable place to cuddle up together. She sat on pillows with her back comfortably against a wall, and I lay across her lap, held in her arms. The rest of the group was continuing with their process and not focused on what we were doing. Louise had a bottle of milk available for me.

I found it surprisingly easy to slip into being one year old. I cried and cried, and it did not sound or feel to me as if I were crying about anything in my present life. It felt like an inexhaustible pool of tears. I felt very little. At the same time that I was being one year old, my Observer self was present and aware. I was not totally "gone." That is a major difference between a planned therapeutic regression in a sane adult, and a psychotic regression. Some part of me knew that I was an adult, that I was in a room full of people, that I was very safe here. But the part of me that was foremost was the baby.

Louise did what a good mother does: she held me, rocked me, and gave me comforting Parent messages. *"It's okay to cry; you are a good girl, I love you, I will take care of you, you are safe here, you are lovable."* I began to feel calmer and my tears subsided. Then I cried hard all over again. Louise decided to feed me from the bottle. I recall two things about the bottle: at first, each drop of milk was the sweetest, most delicious flavor I had ever tasted. I was totally in the present moment, sucking in each separate drop.

But then I felt the urge to cry again, and spit out the nipple. Louise tried to force it back into my lips, and I was surprised by what I experienced next: *rage*. It was an older child self who put inner words to the rage, the essence of which was: *leave me alone, I need to cry, I feel trapped being held; don't try to shut me up!* Of course, the one year old could not articulate any of this, so Louise did not know what was upsetting me, and tried harder to give me the bottle.

When the group took a break, I returned to adulthood (I didn't want to miss out on lunch) and I was able to process with Louise what had happened during our experience of reparenting. The experience had been powerful. I *knew* what it was like for me to be pre-verbal and have someone try to stop a feeling. I believed that I would not have re-experienced that feeling in the same way had I not regressed and been held.

During the following months, I noticed that when my feelings were discounted by someone, I felt irritated but not enraged. It was a welcome shift.

As a beginning TA group leader, I had believed in doing reparenting. I taught people in my groups the value of letting themselves be "little" and of being held, or holding others. This was acceptable in a group setting. The entire concept of the groups was so far removed from ordinary social interaction that groups became a world of their own, where some outside social rules did not apply. If everyone was held at some time or another, it was normal, especially in the free social climate of the '70s.

As the therapist, I found that it was physically uncomfortable for me to hold clients. No matter where I sat, eventually my back would hurt or my arms ache. In group, I could not concentrate fully on one client if I were holding someone else. For the first half of my career I felt vaguely remiss because I was not holding clients and doing reparenting often enough.

Then, during the second half of my career, the social milieu changed, and so did my attitude. As time went on, and I was doing more individual therapy, I found that reparenting techniques were problematic. People were more self-conscious in a one-to-one situation, and felt "silly" doing things that seemed normal in a group. The power of the collective permission of the group was strong and missing from individual sessions. Also, the mainstream therapy world was more vocal about the dangers of touching clients. Now I began to feel guilty about doing exactly what I thought I needed to do more of in prior years. I found that my work was more and more effective without touch or reparenting, other than the verbal kind.

My new stance became a conflict when some of my clients were fledgling therapists who were being trained in groups similar to the ones I had learned in. They came in asking me to hold them as part of the therapy sessions. I refused. We talked about why, what they thought would happen if I did, if I did not, what changes they wanted to make, how else they could accomplish their goals, analyzing the topic *ad nauseam*. Occasionally, when someone did really deep work and was in great distress, I moved closer or put a reassuring hand on her shoulder. (Usually it was a woman. I was more reserved with my male clients.)

Eventually I gave up holding altogether. I simply did not feel comfortable with it. But that was not the end of the debate. I met monthly with a peer group of therapists who all were working with clients who suffered from dissociative disorders, including what was then known as Multiple Personality Disorder (MPD). The client population in general had been severely abused, sometimes tortured, as children.

The psychotherapists in the group held a variety of degrees and came from a variety of training backgrounds. There was a deep split in the group. One side felt it was harmful to touch a client who did not know how to interpret touch (since "positive" touch often had turned, for them, into sexual abuse) and that doing so was anti-therapeutic and unprofessional. The other side felt that a person who had never experienced the warmth and gentleness of "safe" touch needed that to become fully human, and that many of these clients, because of the nature of their dissociative disorder, had no other relationships in which to experience nurturing. They further felt that if a person came to them in the ego state of a terrified child, it was cruel and inhuman not to hold and comfort them. The first group claimed that was not their role, and the comforting could be done through developing inner resources with hypnotic imagery.

I was on the line. I met my first "multiple" client while I was being trained in reparenting, and long before she or I, or my supervisors, knew anything about dissociation. She was already used to the comfort of being held by me. My brief attempt to change that pattern was experienced by her as a cruel rejection by the only person she had ever learned to fully trust. So we continued. I knew that, regardless of theory, it was right for her.

A corollary issue to the touch of reparenting is the end-of-session hug. In the 70's groups (whether sensitivity training, encounter, TA or standard psychotherapy) everyone hugged everyone else at the end of group. The therapist got lots of hugs, too. It was part of the "group culture." It was fun, warm and human. However, I found many complexities in this practice as my clients switched more and more to individual therapy sessions.

A hug communicates a great deal non-verbally. Many of my clients did not know the difference between a social hug and another sort, and their behaviors were sometimes inappropriate. I had clients who added a kiss on the cheek to a hug; clients who patted my back reassuringly as they hugged me; clients, both male and female, who didn't know the boundary between a social hug and one of passion.

There were further complexities. If a client who was accustomed to sharing a final hug with me felt angry at the end of a session, he or she was in a bind about what to do. If I, sensing this, did not initiate the hug, it could have felt like a rejection. If I did, it could have appeared that I was insensitive to the anger. Coming at the end of a session, there was no opportunity to analyze this non-verbal communication, and misunderstandings sometimes occurred. By the following week's session, the subtleties were lost and it was difficult to reconstruct the experience. Transference and counter-transference are complex enough without adding unnecessary elements. I began to appreciate the psychoanalytic viewpoint about non-touch.

While I did not entirely give up hugging with my long-term clients, I learned to be more selective and intuitive about when it felt right. During most of the last decade of my practice I did not introduce holding or hugging with new clients. Happily, I found that the course of treatment progressed very effectively without it.

Doing Group

We sit in a circle on the floor, our backs leaning against a wall or sofa or perhaps a backrest. I, the leader, begin with "Who wants to work?" Sometimes everyone clamors at once; other times, everyone is shy and silent. I wait. I joke, "Okay, who wants to go second?" Someone says, *Me, I'll go*. And so we begin. The work is interactive between the client and me, the group mostly listening, reflecting silently on this person's story, and their own. We work briefly, perhaps 10 or 15 minutes, until there is new awareness, an insight on the part of the client, or until it feels like a natural resting place, a time for her to ponder on her next step. Then it is someone else's turn.

This is what I was taught, in the 1970's, as the TA-Gestalt model of group therapy. It combined the concepts of Transactional Analysis, as developed and written about by Eric Berne and his followers, with many techniques of Gestalt therapy, as developed by Fritz Perls. In the early 1970s, there was an explosion of TA therapy groups across the U.S.

"Doing group" was a phrase idiosyncratic to that era. It conferred a sort of status on the therapist in the early days, and was used in such sentences as, "I can't go to the movies tonight—I'm *doing group* until 10:30p.m.," or "Wednesday is my long day—I do group in the afternoon, and twice more at night." Implicit in these remarks was the image of many people thronging about the therapist. The more groups, and the larger, the more status. Also, the more income. During the years when I "did" several groups a week, I enjoyed the status game.

In those early years of my work, I secretly relished the TA-Gestalt Group model for reasons I had never heard talked about and which I never discussed with anyone. I was "on" all the time. I was very deliberately in defiance of the childhood injunction (a TA term referring to parental rules, spoken and unspoken) from my father, *"Don't try to be the center of attention."* In this model, the leader *is* the center of attention, a limelight shared, of course, with the client. All one's cleverness and creativity can be seen and appreciated by an audience, as opposed to individual therapy, where one's *bon mots* may go unheeded by the distraught client, who is the only other person in the room. The ineptness and errors of the leader are also fully observable, but that did not bother me much. This model of "doing group" appealed to the extrovert, the performer, in me. (For a therapist who is an introvert, it offers a safe opportunity to experiment with another way, under the guise of a therapeutically approved role.) In the TA model which I learned, the therapist is a Leader and the clients know it and revere him/her. There is a great deal of ego-gratification for the therapist, and I loved it.

I never heard anyone say that aloud, and I certainly would never have admitted it, then.

It also, I realized with chagrin some years later, is a masculine model. There is an imbalance of power between the therapist and the group. The power is hierarchical, with the therapist on top of the ladder. The feminist model is more egalitarian, with life experience being more significant than academic degrees. In a feminist group model, as in other styles of group leadership, the role of the therapist is more passive, with the group itself being the therapeutic agent. Other types of groups in which the role of the therapist is more silent and non-directive may include anything from psychoanalytic groups (traditional) to encounter groups (non-traditional).

At a national conference on group therapy which I attended in the early 70s, at the start of my training, I went to a session on leadership styles. The workshop leader, a highly skilled and experienced therapist, posed a most significant question.

"How many of you," she asked, "use a group therapy model in which you work one-to-one with a client within the group setting?" This was the model currently in favor with TA and Gestalt group leaders. About half the hands went up.

"And how many of you use a model in which the group does most of the work and you, as leader, are more passive and non-directive?" The other half of the hands went up.

Then the big question: "How many of you are thinking, while using one model, that you should be using the other?" Almost all the hands went up, with a great deal of self-conscious laughter. I, myself, had that thought, often.

"Each model is fine and has its place," she went on, "so long as you're comfortable and understand what you're doing. Give up the guilt."

Other than gratifying my ego, I loved the TA-Gestalt mixture because its effectiveness for clients was immediately apparent, and because there was a great deal of opportunity for role-play and for drama. Gestalt techniques were highly varied and creative, and often involved utilizing the entire group. Sometimes the therapist gave the client a sentence to repeat, asking her to walk around the circle and say it directly to each person. The sentence would come from the issue being worked on by the client and was tailored to his or her specific need. An example might be that a person who had been told all his life by his family that he would never amount to anything, and who believed it, might be instructed to stand up and say to each group member, "I am important! I *do* count." Said at the right moment, and in a thoughtful way, an experience such as this often had a strong positive, and lasting, impact on the client.

There was also a reflected influence on the other group members. Inevitably, someone else in the room was likely to have the same inner message, and simply hearing it mirrored started the wheels of change turning. Usually as one person worked in some depth, others in the group recognized their own issues, and often volunteered to work next on something that might have taken them months longer to reach in individual therapy. The group provided a permission to move into depth, bypassing the superficial problems of "what do I say to the boss" and moving directly to the issue of recognizing self-worth that lay beneath the question.

In the '70's, groups were "in." Therapy clinics were flooded with phone calls from people wanting to find out who was running a therapy group and whether they could join. Some therapists had groups as large as 30 or 40 people. Many therapists had mix-and-match rules, such as "If you miss a session, since you must pay anyway, you can make it up by coming to one of my other groups." While the groups were beneficial, sometimes they were misused. I once met a young woman who was in three groups run by the same therapist, and she spent her days running from her part-time job to one or another of these groups, each of which lasted for three hours. She was addicted to the "group high." I thought it was sad, a misuse of a potentially good thing. Instead of using group therapy to enhance her life, the groups had *become* her life.

In traditional groups, members are cautioned not to have contact outside the group room. In the TA-Gestalt groups, however, a sense of community grew and outside friendships were not discouraged. I know of people who met in group therapy and 20 years later were still friends.

By the end of the '80's, two new group movements had arisen. Twelve-step programs, starting with Alcoholics Anonymous and expanding to other areas of addictive behaviors, were everywhere. In addition, many topic-oriented support groups had sprung up at churches, hospitals and community centers. There were groups for people considering marriage and those considering divorce, groups for new parents, for working mothers, for bereavement, and for better communication with a partner. Both the Twelve-step groups and the support groups were free and highly effective.

It became more and more difficult to find clients who wanted to be in group therapy. The majority of the therapists I had trained with were, like me, mostly conducting individual sessions. If I mentioned the possibility of group therapy to a client, a common response was, "What would the group be about?" or "Why would I want to do *that*?" Each client had me all to herself for an hour, did not want to give that up, and usually could not afford both individual and group therapy. While some therapists maintained therapy groups by telling clients at the outset that they *must* come twice a week and participate weekly in a group, or they would not take them on, I never felt comfortable with that approach. When my last group, a women's group that stayed together successfully for a year, finally ended, I did not try to organize another.

By that time, I was uncomfortable with the strongly directive approach I had learned and used effectively for so many years. If I were to continue leading therapy groups, I would have had to learn quite another model. Also, because of the logistics of people's work schedules, groups generally had to meet in the evenings or on Saturdays. I, however, had honed down my schedule to four weekdays, ending at 5:30 pm.

Also, I was learning other new things, such as how to recognize and work with severe dissociative disorders. With interests turning in other directions, I ended the era of work with small groups. The phrase "doing group" has not been in my vocabulary for many years. Therapeutically, I may have had some regrets, but semantically speaking, there is no loss at all.

An Aftermath of Childhood Abuse: Discovering MPD

In the summer of 1982, on vacation in Charlevoix, Michigan, I was browsing an outdoor table at a library used-book sale. For just one dollar, I bought a hard-cover book called *Mind in Many Pieces*, by Ralph Allison, MD. It had been published only two years earlier.

The next day, on the beach of Lake Michigan, I read the entire book. It was an account, by a psychiatrist, of his work with multiple personality patients. I was fascinated. All I knew of Multiple Personality Disorder (considered a rare condition when Allison wrote his book) was what I had learned from watching two once-popular movies on the subject, "Sybil" and "The Three Faces of Eve." I had nearly completed my doctoral program in Clinical Psychology. MPD had never emerged as a topic there, or in my prior training groups or in my many case supervision sessions. The stories in this book seemed bizarre, but plausible.

When I returned to my internship placement, I loaned the book to my clinical supervisor. I was eager for another opinion. He was a skilled psychotherapist with a doctorate in Behavioral Psychology. He brought back the book three days later, shaking his head. "Forget it," he said. "I think it is all fiction."

I didn't believe it was fiction. I could not imagine why a psychiatrist would risk his professional credibility by trying to pass off fiction as fact. But I did not feel knowledgeable enough to argue with a supervisor, and the book did not seem to apply to any of my cases. So I put it in the back of my mind, and let it go. For a while.

◆   ◆   ◆

Betty Jean's case had all the elements of a mystery.

She had been my client over a period of eleven years, starting in the early '70s, when I was new to the work of doing psychotherapy. Occasionally Betty Jean, an attractive, athletic career woman in her late 40's, announced that she was through with therapy, but she always returned. During that first eleven years, she had accomplished a great deal: she had stopped drinking, had ended an unhappy marriage and had made advancements in her career. She had a new love in her life and had improved her relationships with each of her three adult children. By these objective standards, her therapy had been successful, although unusually prolonged.

Yet something was not right. Even though her life seemed to be going well, she still experienced sudden, agonizing moments of confusion and terror. It was after another of these episodes, about four months after she had "ended" therapy for the third time, that she phoned me for another appointment.

"Something is wrong and I have no idea what it is," she told me when she was in my office.

I had no idea, either. "We will figure it out together," I promised her. I sounded more confident than I felt.

Betty Jean had been abreacting (reliving early-in-life traumatic experiences) since the beginning of our therapy together. She came to each session dressed in a business suit and high heels. Yet within minutes of entering my office she often looked and sounded like a terrified child. Many traumatic scenes and phrases were repeated over and over in a trance-like state. Often, when she came back to the present moment, she did not remember what she had said or done during the abreaction. It was quite clear to me that she had suffered sexual abuse in her childhood, and was now acting it out in my office. I was at a loss to help her remember or integrate what she was communicating to me, and was unsure if there was any value in letting her re-experience such suffering. However, after such a session, she usually reported feeling a sense of release and relief, and functioned much better in her outer life. Until the next time.

When I had asked other supervisors about the wisdom or value of allowing these abreactions to occur, I was advised to stop them. But Betty Jean seemed to need that release; otherwise, she suffered agonizingly long nights at home and was unable to work during the day. Eventually, I stopped asking, and followed my own instincts.

◆   ◆   ◆

A client named M. worked in a library. One day in 1987, almost five years after I had read the book by Ralph Allison, M. brought me a new book. "I thought this might interest you," she said. "It just came in. I couldn't put it down."

The book was called *When Rabbit Howls* and the author was listed as "the Troops for Trudy Chase." It was the story of the ninety personalities that allegedly existed in one woman, and both the Forward and the Epilogue were written by her therapist, Robert A. Phillips Jr., PhD.

I, too, could not put the book down. I knew that when a client brings in a book, that book is delivering a message about the person who brought it. But I could not, then, identify it with M. Throughout its pages, it was Betty Jean's image that stayed with me.

I became, temporarily, obsessed with this book, and with a growing question: could Betty Jean's symptoms be due to MPD? And if so, what did I need to do to help her?

One spring day, about a week after finishing the book, I took off from work to attend a seminar on family therapy. Like most seminars, it took place in a hotel conference room with no windows. I was ambivalent about being indoors when the weather was finally so pleasant, but since I had canceled appointments and paid my fee, I decided to go.

It was the right decision, and it had nothing to do with family therapy. The first person I saw when I walked in was Dr. B., a former supervisor toward whom I had felt respect and affection. I had been in supervision with her during my official internship placement at the psychology clinic of a local university; she had also been the consultant to the private clinic where I worked. I was pleased when she invited me to sit at her lunch table. She congratulated me on having completed my doctoral work, and we exchanged stories about our current lives.

Then, trying to sound only casually obsessed, I told Dr. B. and others at the table about *When Rabbit Howls*. No one else had heard of it yet. Privately, I asked Dr. B. if she remembered my having discussed with her, during our earlier contacts, a client who had frequent abreactions. Because we were in a public place I did not want to go into detail or mention the name of the client. She recalled the case only vaguely; our supervision sessions had occurred several years earlier. I told her about Betty Jean's recent terror and return to therapy, and about how much her symptoms came to mind when I read *Rabbit*.

Then came the most important information. "I know a woman you must contact," Dr. B. told me. "Here's her card." She dug into her purse, found her wallet, and pulled out a business card.

"I heard her speak last week, purely by accident," she went on. "My mail got delivered to the wrong office. I went upstairs to get it and this woman, Carol, was there to give a talk on MPD. Only one other person had showed up and my next client had cancelled, so I stayed to listen. She's worked with MPD patients for a long time, and is going all over the city to educate therapists. Call her!"

Coincidences: that M. worked in a library; that Dr. B. and I were at this conference together; that Dr. B's mail was delivered to the wrong office; that her client canceled just when Carol was speaking on MPD. I went home so excited about the new information that I scarcely remembered what the family therapy conference was about.

I called Carol, and she returned my call that evening. "I need to know more about MPD," I implored her. "What do I do next?"

Carol gave me some book titles. At that time, the professional literature was sparse. I told her some of Betty Jean's symptoms. She invited me to come on the following Friday to a meeting for therapists working with MPD.

I was almost as excited as before my first training session. At last, perhaps, I would find the help *I* needed to give Betty Jean the help *she* needed. I bought the books and devoured every word. I went to the Friday meeting. About twenty-five therapists were present, from all over SE Michigan. Some had traveled for two hours to get there. A few were fairly experienced at working with MPD; others, like myself, were experienced therapists but new to understanding dissociation. Carol gave a brief presentation, followed by an open discussion and question/answer time.

I was full of questions: *How will I know? How do I let her know? What do I do differently if this is true?*

The chief bit of advice I came away with was: *Don't rush it. If she's multiple, she'll let you know. Just start looking for clues.*

Having known Betty Jean for eleven years, I did not feel I was rushing. If anything, I wanted to hurry. But I did not want to frighten her, or make a misdiagnosis. I learned, from my reading and from the group, that one of the signs that a client may be multiple is being in therapy for many years and not truly making progress. Betty Jean had made outward progress, but her subjective world was still as chaotic as ever. I was warned that after the diagnosis is made, there is a period of intensified inner chaos, because the life-long secret is out, and all the alters react. I wanted to help ease her chaos, not to add to it. I decided I would have to wait and see.

◆   ◆   ◆

Betty Jean made it easy for me. At the first session after I had attended the group meeting, but before I had said anything about MPD, she said, "I have to tell you something strange. I feel like there are other people inside of me."

The synchronicity of this revelation did not escape me, but I chose to keep that to myself for now. "Tell me more about what that is like," I said.

"Yesterday I was in the kitchen. I felt like two other people were having a conversation. But no one was there, only me. This has happened a lot, recently. Am I going crazy, or what?"

"Were the voices inside your head, or outside?" I asked. Multiples experience voices as inside; schizophrenics experience voices as coming from outside of themselves.

She paused, was thoughtful. "They were inside," she said slowly, "the same as the sound of a little child crying. I've started to hear that, too." She looked at me intently, looking strong and determined. "I want to get to the bottom of this. I want to know what is going on. I have other people inside. I can hear them all the time, now." Then she looked frightened. "Are you sure I'm not crazy?" she asked.

"You are not crazy," I was now able to tell her with confidence. "Those 'voices' are all parts of you that you split off so you wouldn't have to remember painful events. From now on, our work together will be about introducing you to them and them to each other, and getting you put back into one whole person."

She smiled with relief and gratitude.

One of the first mysteries we solved was about her name. Betty Jean was the name on the check she gave me each week. I had noticed for a long time, however, that she was inconsistent about the use of the names "Betty" and "Jean." When she began therapy, she introduced herself as Betty. Several years later, she preferred being called Jean. Whenever I asked her questions about her name, as I did many times, over the years, (*What are you called at work? What does your husband call you? What were you called at home as a child? What did other kids call you? Which name do you prefer? What meaning does each name hold for you?*) she was vague and inconsistent in her mumbled answers. Usually she said, "It doesn't make any difference."

At last this confusion began to clear. Another alter (a split-off part of the personality) emerged. This part had been around since early childhood as an inner helper (her name, in fact, was 'Friend'). Friend told me that 'Betty' was the name the father called her when he wanted her to get down to the basement where the abuse took place. 'Jean' was the name the family called her when she was upstairs. Jean and Betty went through life each unaware of the existence of the other, or of the life circumstances of the other. Betty remained fixated in childhood, and remembered much of the physical, sexual and emotional trauma that was perpetrated upon her. (There were still other child alters created by Betty to carry the worst memories.) Jean, by contrast, went to school, remembered going on pleasant excursions with her father, finished college, married and raised a family. However, she could feel the 'Betty' emotion and pain all her life, without understanding what it was or where it came from. When she was too incapacitated to function, 'Friend' came out and helped her through situations.

My initial reaction to the discovery that MPD was the key to the puzzle of Betty Jean was excitement. Through the study group, I was being introduced to an entirely new way of conceptualizing the human mind and theories that were on the cutting edge of our knowledge of consciousness. I read every piece of literature on MPD that I could get my hands on. Everything I learned about MPD fit with my prior experience of Betty Jean. Here was an entirely new focus, one which should make it possible for me to truly and effectively help Betty Jean to get better. I was hopeful that her problems would reach a quick resolution.

I was wrong.

The work was much more intricate and complex than I could have imagined. Although in many ways her outer life continued to improve, the next five years of therapy were the most difficult she had endured. The memories of abuse that arose as Betty was finally able to speak were almost too traumatic for her to endure or for Jean to take in. Her inner chaos and anxiety increased. She repeatedly reported to me that when she awoke in the morning, her bedclothes were in a tangle on the floor and the teddy bear she (Betty) slept with was thrown wildly across the room. Jean had no memory of any of this occurring. In the morning she felt exhausted. Rather than uncovering and integrating memories and alters, as I had hoped would happen, I had to slow down the process so that Jean could function in her public and working life.

There were some positive aspects of this phase of work with Betty Jean that balanced the painful discoveries. Jean no longer carried Betty's heavy depression all the time. This enabled her to become a dynamic force at work, and gain a major promotion. She began more often to go out socially with friends. Once Betty was known to Jean, I helped Jean learn how to accept and then take emotional care of the 'Betty' part of herself. During one session, Jean reported that she had played golf during the week and Betty enjoyed riding in the golf cart.

A puzzling physical symptom arose, however. Whenever a memory of the father came up in the session, Betty Jean experienced stabbing pains around the heart and on the left side of her back. She interpreted this as "he broke my heart." But despite her therapeutic insights, the pain persisted. I consulted my study group. Colleagues believed Betty Jean's pain was either a body-memory of being injured, or that her insight about the broken heart explained it. However, as the pain continued I was not convinced it was only a metaphor. I insisted she see her doctor.

It was lung cancer.

In the view of Jean and her alter, Friend, this illness was created by a group of inner personalities who wanted to die. (One was Betty, the abused child; one was Irene, an inner copy of her depressed mother; a third alter, whose energy was felt by all of them, was named Despair.) Jean was not a reader of articles on holistic medicine or mind-body psychology. This was her intuitive "knowing." I tend to feel she was right, although it was also true that earlier in her life she had been a heavy smoker. Betty Jean died several months after the cancer diagnosis and before her dissociative issues were resolved.

I asked her, after the cancer had been diagnosed, whether she thought she would have been better off if we had not uncovered the MPD.

"No," she said, "this had to be. It's been a living hell at times, but in many ways my life is so much richer. I think this is how God wanted it to be."

"Well," I said, "I just wish I'd known about all this ten years ago."

"No," she said emphatically, "that would've been too soon. Jean had to get strong first. We did it just right."

Mystery and Controversy

The stories I relate here date back more than a decade from this writing, in 2004; yet there are still no definitive answers to any of the issues raised. The world, both inside and outside the profession of psychotherapy, is still divided; studies are still being done and refuted with counter-studies, and the mysteries continue. I report my experiences because I find the questions fascinating and don't think they will go away soon. The controversies include the existence of satanic cults, past lives, alien abductions, channeled information and false memories. I have no answers and stand firmly in the middle on all issues. I urge new therapists who unexpectedly encounter clients who present with any of these issues to keep an open mind and know that they are not struggling alone.

◆   ◆   ◆

It is October, 1989. I am sitting in a large auditorium in the Hyatt Regency in downtown Chicago, surrounded by at least 400 other therapists from all over the U.S. We have gathered to attend a conference on Dissociative Disorders, including what was then labeled Multiple Personality Disorder. On the stage is the conference convener and host, a well respected psychiatrist, Dr. B. He is lecturing about the signs and icons of satanic cults, displaying them with an overhead projector onto a screen. I glance around: people's heads are nodding in recognition, like wheat waving in a field.

Dr. B. asks, "How many of you are working with MPD patients who were or are victims of a satanic cult?" I am astonished to see about three quarters of the people in the room raise their hands.

I have had no experience or contact with clients connected with satanic cults, but many of my colleagues have clients who have reported this phenomenon. According to the information they received from their clients, which matches the information being disseminated from the stage at the Hyatt, these cults are composed of people who "pass" as high level citizens: teachers, doctors, judges, policemen, ministers, attorneys. Because of their double roles, they can maintain the secrecy: when investigators come around, they can protect themselves by lying. They meet in hidden cellars, follow certain rituals, such as wearing robes, observe ordinary holidays but giving them sinister meanings, and perform bizarre acts, such as sacrifices of animals and children. These cults are said to be interconnected rather than random, part of a centuries old system of evil around the globe.

Many of the diagnosed cases of MPD involve young people who, independently of one another, report childhoods in families who were part of cults. When a child escapes and grows up to tell the tale, she is not believed. Except by her therapist.

What is this about? I sit in my seat in that huge auditorium, dumbfounded. If it is true, why haven't these cults been discovered by the police, the FBI, the news media? Why are the members of my profession the holders of such horrible secret information? And if it is not true, what is the source of the stories being told to hundreds of therapists in private offices all around the world? Why are *we* the only repositories of such shattering information?

I am totally bewildered.

◆   ◆   ◆

I am in a posh restaurant at a luncheon with a colleague who is very excited about her newly formed professional contact with Brian Weiss, MD, a psychiatrist who has written several books about the past life experiences of his clients. My colleague similarly has many clients who come to her specifically to be hypnotized and to induce past life experiences. Through her work alone and with Brian Weiss, she has had memories of what she believes to be some of her own past lives. Apart from this subject, my friend is a well balanced, attractive mother, wife, grandmother; she has worked successfully for many years with children, both normal and disturbed, as well as with couples and families. She is bright, energetic, and holds a PhD in Educational Psychology. She is not a "kook."

I am feeling somewhat uncomfortable discussing this topic at a luncheon, which is actually a bridal shower for the daughter of a mutual friend of ours, also a psychologist. I am interested in what she is relating, but I would prefer to hear about this in private, not here, where I feel our professional reputations could be tarnished. However, it is clear that she is very excited about the topic and wants to raise it for general discussion. The other women at the table do not pick up on it (fortunately, from my perspective) and the subject is dropped.

I consider making an appointment with her for myself.

◆   ◆   ◆

A friend urges me to read a book called *Abduction*, by John E. Mack, MD. The author is a Harvard Medical School psychiatrist and has already won a Pulitzer Prize for an earlier work. His credentials are in order. This book is an account of stories told to him by 13 of the 72 people who have come to see him to recover memories, under hypnosis, of alien abductions. He tries to be scientifically objective. It is clear that he believes them. There is some small amount of objective evidence to corroborate their stories. He makes a plea that science not remain "scientific" by ignoring data that don't fit into their too-narrow scheme of understanding.

As with the cult phenomena: I do not know if I believe or disbelieve (in the existence of satanic cults or of alien beings from other galaxies). But I do believe that when evidence exists that does not fit the accepted paradigm, it is not rational or scientific to deal with it by ignoring it or by ridicule.

◆   ◆   ◆

One of my clients has developed the ability to be a "channel." An "entity" that is not a part of herself communicates with her telepathically and she, in a self-induced trance state, can deliver his message. Sometimes she hears and remembers the words, and sometimes not, depending on the privacy of the message. At first I believed these words to come from a more highly functioning part of her own personality. There was always a great deal of wisdom imparted, and my task, as I saw it, was to help her to hear and retain that wisdom in her own life and relationships. It came from her, to her, and belonged to her.

On a few occasions, at the end of a session, the words that came forth were meant for me, and were picking up on a thought that was unspoken but in my mind, and not known by my client. This gave me pause. Is my client that highly psychic? Is there another "entity," an energy formation, which can be heard and felt but not seen? If I saw him/it, would I think I was hallucinating? Would I be right?

◆   ◆   ◆

Alternative explanations exist for the phenomena of belief in satanic cults, alien abductions, past life memories and channeling. The explanations are as controversial as the subjects they are trying to explain.

Two of the chief theories are false memory and cultural myth.

False memory holds that we distort the actual facts of an occurrence, or can be made to believe something actually happened when it did not occur at all. This has been indicated through experiments in which people are told stories under hypnosis until they believe they really happened. Certainly I can attest, in my every day life, to the prevalence of false memories in myself. One example is that earlier in this chapter I said that something was shown with an overhead projector. Even as I remembered that with a picture in my mind, the picture changed to one of a large cardboard display being held up to the audience. Common sense argued that the auditorium was too large to use anything but a projector, so I went with that image. If I had to testify to that in a court of law as being the absolute truth, I would have great difficulty.

On another recent occasion, I began to tell my husband a rather bizarre story that I said I had heard from a friend. My husband, an attorney, interrupted me with, "You are telling me the facts of the legal case I told you about yesterday." I, being certain in my mind that the friend had told me this story, said, "You mean you both know the same people?"

"No," he said a bit impatiently, "*I* told you that story. It is my case."

I had to prove him wrong, so I phoned my friend. I could picture talking to her the day before, and knew precisely what part of the kitchen I was standing in when we spoke. I said, "Remember the story you told me yesterday about the family who…" and I repeated the facts.

"Who?" my friend said. "What are you talking about? I never told you that story. I don't know anyone like that."

That is how false memory works.

But, say the defenders of the reality of traumatic recall, memory works differently in the case of trauma. It is stored and retrieved in a different part of the brain from ordinary memory. It is recalled in small, vivid pieces, like tiny links in a jigsaw puzzle, often triggered by a present sensory stimulus such as the sight of someone's beard or the smell of smoke, which reminds the brain of the long-buried sensation. Several studies using new techniques of brain imaging attest to this difference.

The mystery to me, and to the researchers in what is called Post-Traumatic Stress Disorder (PTSD), is why more research in this important area of knowledge is not being done. PTSD affects hundreds of thousands of lives: not only abused children, but also war veterans, and survivors of earthquakes, holocausts, rape, fire, attempted murder and other horrors...you get the picture. These memories are too overwhelming to carry in their entirety: they go underground, only to resurface incompletely as "flashbacks" at inopportune moments, creating tremendous anxiety, stress and disruption to the lives of the survivors.

"Oh, yes," say the false memory people, ignoring this data, "but under hypnosis, anyone can be made to believe anything. And with all the stories in newspapers, magazines, movies and on TV about cults and aliens and entities, anyone's imagination can carry the memory of things they have read or heard."

At this point the sociologists join in. "When a story is told enough times," they tell us, "it becomes a rumor, and then it spreads and becomes a cultural myth. All of these phenomena—cults, aliens and channeled spirits—are cultural myths."

But where did the myths begin? Each person who became a client had been traumatized by remembered events. Many of these were *not* recovered under hypnosis, but were recalled outside of therapy sessions, or before entering therapy at all. Each person believed that he was the only one to whom this particular horror had occurred, and told the story to a therapist who could see and feel the reality of the client's terror. Initially, each therapist had not heard of these events: prior to the mid or late '80's, none of us were trained to know about satanic cults or alien abductions. *Much of this material came out in therapy sessions in the years <u>before</u> there were books on the subject, or articles in all the media.* The clients felt like isolated victims and the therapists were empathic if sometimes skeptical listeners.

The amount of emotion generated on both sides of this phenomenon is intense and sometimes irrational. Therapists can react to the mere suggestion of the possibility that perhaps a reported trauma did not actually happen to one of their clients the way a mother would react if someone accused her child of lying. Two events in which I participated attest to that.

The first happened in a professional study group to which I belonged, which was connected with the International Society for the Study of Dissociation (ISSD), the same organization that gave the conference I mentioned at the start of this chapter. It was two or three years after that conference when the ISSD newsletter carried an article by a well-respected leader of the society, urging therapists not to talk publicly about satanic cults as if they were established facts. He did not take a stand for or against the existence of cults; only stated that the organization (ISSD) was already controversial enough because of dealing with the phenomenon of Multiple Personality Disorder; it did not help the situation to speak of something unproved as if it were incontrovertibly true.

I was very glad to see that editorial: I agreed with it completely. At the next local meeting of our group, I decided to bring it to the attention of the group, some of whom did not subscribe to the newsletter. A number of therapists in the group were working with clients who reported being cult survivors.

What I thought was an objective reporting of an article on my part was met with hoots of derision from those who were treating these cult survivors. A heated debate ensued. I found myself ostracized: several people would not give me so much as a nod at the coffee break. And, a month or two later, the group acted the way a "multiple personality" does when in stress: they split. The "cult survivor" therapists formed their own group which met an hour earlier, so that they could discuss therapeutic issues without including anyone who might doubt the existence of an international conspiracy.

In a way, I knew exactly what they were experiencing: it was how I felt when a colleague had suggested that the woman I was helping through her own multiple personality syndrome was, in fact, only borderline and depressed, since MPD really did not exist. I decided I would never discuss cases with *her* again!

◆   ◆   ◆

A second experience of hot emotions occurred at another conference, held locally, with about 250 therapists in attendance. The topic was False Memory Syndrome. The keynote speaker was a woman from another state, a psychology professor who gave a very scholarly paper on the topic of memory and trauma. At the end of her speech, she made a personal digression: she had recently recalled abuse in her own life, had recalled it after two or three therapy sessions, without hypnosis. She had gone home to confront her parents.

The parents, she told us, responded with anger and denial. They sent letters attacking her credibility to the University department that was about to grant her tenure; they also made a public plea to other parents who had been "falsely" accused. The public plea had a huge response, from which the speaker's mother founded an organization with a pseudo-scientific title: the False Memory Syndrome Association (FMSA). The speaker's parents were not scientists or psychologists. They were, the speaker said, lying.

The audience of therapists, I among them, gave the woman a standing ovation. I was moved by her sincerity, her willingness to be vulnerable in a professional setting, and the similarity of her story to those of my own clients. The audience believed her. We had all read about the FMSA, an organization which had publicly attacked the integrity of our profession by claiming that psychotherapists hypnotized patients and made them "remember" abuse that had never actually occurred. Hearing how the FMSA began, from a psychologist with much to lose by being so frank in this setting, felt like an historically important event.

The next speaker was a psychiatrist with impeccable credentials in the field of dissociation. He had traveled from Georgia to be with us in Michigan. Although the conference conveners clearly had felt that he had something to add to the discussion of memory, the man didn't have a chance: he was on the advisory board of FMSA, and, before he even spoke, was *persona non grata* with the very partisan audience. Although he claimed not to be taking sides in this controversy, he was barely listened to. He received hostile questions and very little applause. I felt sorry for him, and embarrassed by the rudeness of the group. He looked like a kind man.

◆　　◆　　◆

Satanic cults. Past lives. Aliens, spaceships, and channeled entities. Memories, real or false. Psychotherapists have become the holders of reports of these experiences, which so drastically alter the world view and the lives of those to whom they occur. It seems to be up to each of us, in our small office cubicles, alone with one survivor, and collectively as a profession, with our thousands of patients, to figure out the mystery of what it all means. Nothing in our formal education ever prepared us for that.

I wish I had more information, more advice to offer. In the years since I attended the events mentioned here, there has been more literature, more debate, and more reports of events that do not fit the consensus reality of the larger population. But there are still no definitive answers to the question of what is real and what is imagined.

Certainly, there are instances where hypnosis has been improperly used to create false memories. There are people who truly hallucinate, who see and hear things that are not real. There are people who have read the many books now available on each of these topics and who fabricate stories. On the other hand, we also know that childhood abuse occurs, with disastrous consequences. It is in the newspapers every day. We have legal evidence of cults, although they may not be satanic or part of an international network. Thousands of sane, rational people have experiences that are not part of most people's every-day reality but which are life-transforming. Such experiences may include memories of abuse or cult rituals; they may be such phenomena as out-of-body travel or receiving a visit from a loved one who has passed on; they may include spontaneous memories of what seems to be a past life, or an unexpected physical healing.

The question for me as a therapist is: what do I do when someone enters my office with a story I find difficult to corroborate; with an experience I have never had myself? Must I believe that anyone who reports an unusual experience is either lying or crazy? To what extent is my own perception of reality limited by the cultural consensus? How do I respond when I cannot know what is true?

The limited answer I have come to, through my own experience, is to listen with respect. I do not have to be a judge. I can help the client explore the meaning of his experience; refer him to books that deal with the topic; look at the situation as if it were a metaphor or a myth. I need to be watchful: if this person is psychotic, it will show up in other behaviors and thought patterns. In that case, I would I turn to standard treatments for psychotic behavior.

However, if she or he is a well functioning, balanced person in most areas of life, I may be called upon to stretch my own limited belief system. If I cannot do so with integrity, I will refer the client to someone who can be more accepting of her reality. I do not need to make someone else's reality more painful by assuming I know more than she about her experience.

No one has all the answers to mystery in life. As long as mystery exists, there will be controversy. My job as a therapist, as I see it, is to remain open, respectful and clear-headed in the face of questions which, even in the 21st century, remain ambiguous.

PART V

Saying Goodbye

Letting Go

I am in a session with a client with whom I have worked for over two years. During that time, she has come out of her depression, improved her relationships with her husband and children and has decided to return to college to finish a degree. I observe that her entire demeanor seems brighter again today than in past months: her posture more upright, her smile more spontaneous, her eyes more alive. The thought crosses my mind, *She doesn't need to come for therapy much longer.*

I return my attention to what my client is telling me: she and her husband are planning their first trip away from the children in ten years. This is a significant event, one which she has spent much therapy time exploring. My own thought, about her termination, flickers on again. When she says, a few minutes later, "I've been thinking of stopping therapy," I am not surprised.

What does surprise me is my mixed inner response. I am pleased that she brought up the topic of ending therapy. Had I been the one, it might have felt to her like a rejection as much as an affirmation of her growth. I am pleased at the synchronicity; the reality of ending came to both of us at the same time. But I also feel disappointment: I have thoroughly enjoyed the sessions with this woman and I already feel the loss. She has been a cooperative and gratifying person to work with, has worked hard and put new behaviors into practice with positive results. She has been a consistent and reliable customer, coming every week at 2:00p.m. Now, as well as losing the relationship, I will be faced with a gap in my schedule and, I hate to admit, in my income.

My inner thoughts and feelings flash through me like a gentle wave, and recede. None of this is relevant or appropriate to my client. My outer response is more along the lines of, "Tell me what you have been thinking about this," said with an approving nod of my head and in a tone which, I hope, conveys interest.

She tells me, sometimes prompted by more questions from me, how long she has thought of ending therapy, how much better she is feeling now, how she and her husband want to be sure they have the funds for their vacation, how sad she is when she thinks about stopping her visits, the anxiety she feels about making this decision, how scared she has been for several weeks to bring it up, how relieved that I am not angry: these are some of the many issues that arise for most clients in regard to the issue of ending therapy.

I suggest to her that we take a few more sessions to explore each of these issues, so that when she does leave, it will be with a sense of well being over having made a decision that is right for her, at the right time. She agrees to this, and sets up another appointment. We make it for two weeks from now instead of the usual one week. The separation process has begun.

The next day, at a meeting with my colleagues, I explore my own ambivalence about this event. The four of us meet every Tuesday at lunch time to discuss triumphs and difficulties in our work, and to offer suggestions to one another. This day, we are in the office next to mine, a large, sunny room with comfortable sofas and a coffee table filled with low-calorie food to share: grapes, humus and pita, strawberries, cut-up carrots and celery sticks, non-fat chocolate cookies. We fill our paper plates as we talk.

It turns out that everyone in our peer consultation group currently has a client who either just terminated, or is in the process of doing so. Someone brings up the topic of worry about lost income. "Three people are leaving this month," she tells us, "and one of them came two times a week. I'm worried. New clients are calling less often now that so many people have free care with their HMO's." Others express their concern about the same issue. Then someone turns the topic to the sense of satisfaction she feels when someone has clearly made progress after months of hard inner work. "It's like helping your kids learn to walk, or read, or drive a car," she muses. "You know that they made the shift from trying to mastery, but you also know that you played some part in it. And you feel so good, for them and for yourself."

"And just when you are enjoying them, they're gone," someone adds. "A person has a problem, he comes to you for help, you like him, you help him, and he leaves you. What kind of a job *is* this, anyway?"

It strikes me how much saying goodbye to a client is like what I went through in the process of raising and letting go of my own children. From weaning them to sending them off to college, at each new juncture I experienced a mixture of pleasure and regret, pride and loss, relief and sadness. The positive side had to do with recognizing and applauding the healthy growth in them and the new freedom that gave me. The "down" side was related to the difficulty of saying goodbye to a stage of relationship which, for me, had been rewarding and now would no longer exist.

There is a major difference, of course, between parenting and being a psychotherapist in regard to letting go. With my children, the relationships continued in a new form. With a client, I am saying goodbye not to a stage of relationship, but to the relationship itself. Regardless of how much I may like this person, the relationship is not going to evolve into an out-of-the-office friendship. That is both impractical and unethical. The professional relationship needs to remain that way even after the client stops coming into the office. There is always the possibility that in a year or two some unforeseen life event will make it desirable for this person to return to treatment. It is unfair to the client not to keep the therapeutic relationship intact.

The complexities of the "letting go" process have long intrigued me. I chose, some years earlier, to write my doctoral dissertation on the experience that women have when their last child leaves home. At the time, my youngest child had just left for college. I was seeking the commonalties of the situation, and found that all the women I interviewed experienced not only ambivalence, but surprise when they encountered the opposite side of what they had expected. Those expecting loss found it but also, somewhat guiltily, admitted to finding relief and freedom; those who could hardly wait until their kids were out of the house were surprised at the sadness they also felt.

And so it was for me when a client was truly ready to leave therapy. It meant I had done my job well. Ironically, the therapist's reward for good work is to become unnecessary.

A therapist with unresolved ego needs, abandonment issues or simple greed can undermine the therapeutic process by convincing the client he or she needs to stay longer. Sometimes, of course, he is leaving prematurely and truly *does* need to stay on. But I am not talking about that situation. Let's assume the work is, for the client, complete. The therapist who has a problem letting go might say, to the detriment of the newly discovered confidence of the client: "Leaving now would be the *worst* thing you could do." Or "What makes you think you are ready so soon?" Or *"Really?"* uttered in a tone of surprise, as if this were the most incredulous pronouncement imaginable. Or, "Yes, you *did* manage to get a job. But what about the fact that you always antagonize someone into firing you? How will you handle *that*?" Or, "You know, when you started here, I told you the therapy would take at least seven years. If you stop coming, I will continue to charge you for missed sessions." (No, I didn't make that one up; I knew of someone who actually said that to a client who wanted to leave.) I'm sure a creative therapist could think of even more ways to make it clear that leaving is not an acceptable thing to do. Short of sobbing, "No, don't leave me," that is.

Some therapists and schools of therapy consider termination of treatment to be a hard-line event: once you are done, there is no returning. I have never believed that was necessary or helpful. I always leave open the option of returning if a new situation arises that feels difficult to handle or to figure out alone. I also leave open the option of contacting me by letter or phone. This may be a way of avoiding the pain of a final farewell, both on my part and on behalf of my client, but it also seems to me eminently human. When someone ends therapy with a major life event ahead, I care enough to want to know how it turns out, and I want my client to know that I care. *Was the baby born healthy? Did you complete your Master's degree? Are you moving across the country?*

"If it feels right to you, call and let me know," I may invite someone. For me to make the call would violate the post-therapeutic boundary. My ex-client might have a need *not* to talk to me. I can only issue the invitation.

Generally my clients are very happy to know that although therapy is over, they need not mourn my loss as though I had died. I am still there, and still interested in the next chapter in their lives, if they want to share it.

It is now the agreed upon final session of the woman who is ending therapy, taking a trip with her husband, and returning to college in the fall. The last few sessions, spread out over two week intervals, were used to explore the issues she had raised previously in regard to leaving therapy, as well as one that took her by surprise: the impending loss of relationship with me triggered unfinished grieving over the death of a close friend. Now, both of us feel clear that she is making the right decision at the right time. Today, in this final session, I guide her toward looking at how far she has come since she began her journey with me, where she is now, and what she sees in the months or years ahead. I ask her what stands out for her as having been of most help in our work together. I share with her my view of her therapeutic progress and emphasize the strengths that she has which moved her toward her goal.

As she rises to leave for the last time, we share a hug. She cries as she thanks me. My own tears don't flow until she is out the door. But they are brief: my next client is already in the waiting room. I need to review my notes from his last session before he comes in. I find a Kleenex, and search the file drawer for his folder.

What I Learned from my Clients

I may never know exactly what my clients learned from me. But I can tell you for certain what I learned from them. As I look back over the years I see a long procession of people, entering my various offices one at a time, each bringing me a teaching as tangible as a wrapped package left inside my door, to be opened and studied at leisure. These gifts of knowledge helped me to expand my horizons even as I was helping my clients to expand theirs.

I learned much about the world of work beyond my own. I learned to suspend judgment and social prejudice as my clients led me through worlds I had read about but never entered myself. I learned from their stories what it was like to be a corporate executive with an alcohol problem; a middle manager trying to rise, but saddled with a supervisor who gave unfair evaluations. I learned how difficult it was to be gay in a corporation where revelation of that could cost one's job. A beautiful young graduate engineer explained to me why she worked as a topless dancer: the sole support of two children, she could earn as much in a year of dancing as in ten years of engineering work. She told me how she protected her safety; I learned to suspend my prejudices.

I learned about the world of addictions: to casino gambling, credit card overspending, alcohol, cocaine, sex, food, sports betting. As I worked to help each client understand and control his destructive impulses, I was learning the complexities of money management and mismanagement, the inside bar scene, the way drugs were obtained and how they were used. Sometimes the addict was not my client, but was the client's spouse or lover: then I learned how devastating it is to love someone who is addicted.

I learned about the world of childhood abuse from those who had survived it. I learned of the variety of atrocities that twisted or evil adults could perpetrate on small children and saw for myself how the early wounds warped their adult lives. It was not the same kind of learning that I obtained from reading similar accounts in the daily paper or weekly newsmagazines, or even from reading novels, textbooks or case studies. The survivor sat before me, her raw pain pouring into my room, my heart. As she relived her world, she took me with her as witness.

I learned how the mind fragments when a child is abused and how painful and confusing it is to live with that dysfunction, hour to hour, as an adult. I was given the gift of witnessing the courage of those who stayed with the treatment process, which could be nearly as painful as the original trauma.

I learned new areas of compassion. Although I had been trained to teach all my clients the difference between *I can't* and *I won't*, I learned to recognize real limits to human will and choice. When depression gripped some people so that they said "I *can't* (take a shower, make the phone call, go for a walk)," I finally learned that, indeed, a mental state can be as crippling as a physical paralysis. I was no longer so smug as to insist that I knew better.

I learned that there are some people for whom the act of getting through a day is so difficult, even with antidepressants and years of therapy, that despite their high intelligence and innate kindness, and my incorrigible optimism, they may probably never lead normal, functional lives. Further, I learned to respect their bravery in trying to unravel the mystery of their own development.

I learned patience: to think I knew the answer was never as useful as to guide someone to find her own answer. Looking up the solution to the equation in the back of the book and telling someone does not teach him how to solve it. Sometimes the work took months, or even years, longer than we both wanted it to, but it was worth the wait. For both of us.

I learned how little we know, ultimately, about the intricacies and resilience of the human mind and soul.

I learned that no amount of advice is useful unless the other person really is open to hearing it.

I learned how terribly hard it is to go through a divorce, even for the one seeking it; to be a single parent; to maintain a viable marital relationship against the demands of young children and two full time jobs.

I learned that deep listening is often more effective than giving advice, that bearing witness to another's grief helps lighten the burden, that offering theoretical knowledge is pertinent to the healing process only when leavened with respect, caring and presence.

In addition to these teachings, I received other kinds of gifts.

My clients brought the gift of sharing with me their trust, their openness and their vulnerability, as well as the pain that had been wrapped up, hidden from the world and often from themselves for so many years. I learned to sense that pain beneath the wrapping, to encourage the client to remove the tape and open the box.

I received the gift of watching others improve their lives, finding pleasure where there had been only pain, learning to behave in ways that were life enhancing rather than self-destructive, recognizing and accepting their own feelings, learning to think in new and more useful patterns.

I learned to see beyond the facade and to love the soul. In allowing me to touch their souls, my clients touched mine.

Each person who crossed the threshold of my room left something unique. These gifts are a part of me. Many times a day I unwrap one or another, and find they gleam. My life is filled with riches.

How I Said Goodbye

Saying goodbye as I ended my practice was a long process. It began as I renewed my final lease: I had an intuition that a five-year renewal was too long for me, and requested of my office mates that it be for three years only.

We were standing in the waiting room of our office, the three of us, and my two dear friends and colleagues looked at me with loving sadness in their eyes. Even as we were beginning a new phase together, they knew that for me it was the final one.

"The office won't be the same without you," Sara said. Gayle nodded in agreement. We stood quietly for a moment, then looked at our watches and dispersed to our separate rooms.

At that moment, seeing the depth of reaction of these two women, whom I would continue to see socially outside of the office, to an event still three years away, I knew that my clients, who would *not* see me again, would have a variety of reactions and would need time to process them so that my departure could be a healthy learning situation about how to handle loss.

At that moment I did not feel sadness; I felt a sense of excitement and a determination to enjoy the next three years. I also knew that I could stay longer; a five-year commitment would have made me feel locked in, but signing up for three years felt freeing and did not eliminate the possibility of changing my mind.

I had already reduced my work-schedule from five days a week to four. I proceeded to continue the reduction over the next two years, a half-day at a time. I made a conscious decision about which days and hours I wanted to be in the office, and marked my non-office time in my appointment book as diligently as I wrote down hourly appointments. Keeping to my own schedule decision was a matter of being able to say *No* to others and of believing that my self-commitment to 'time-off' was a valid one.

The two reasons for overloading my schedule which had been operative earlier in my career no longer felt important. The first had been about making more money. Financially, I was now comfortable, had built up a solid retirement account, and did not need the excess income which, added to my husband's, only put us in a higher tax bracket. The second motivator for working beyond my limits was the ego-gratification of having an overly full caseload. Now, at this later stage of my life, my ego needs felt satiated. It was far more important to me to have longer stretches of quiet, unstructured time. The only justification for expanding my office hours was when a client was truly in crisis; then I was quite willing to schedule an extra session.

There were times when I had to say *No* to new clients who sounded really interesting, and times when I worried that such refusals, combined with clients who were leaving, would cause my practice to end sooner than I wanted it to. However, this did not happen, and the three years wound down quite gradually to three day weeks, and later two days. The final year, I took no new clients at all, referring all new callers to others, and the final six months there were no calls from new clients, only from former ones returning to have a few final sessions before I left.

About a year before I was ready to leave, I told my clients the news. If termination is a difficult decision for a client to make, the situation of a therapist leaving (whether due to retirement, illness or moving away) is even more difficult, because it is a reality over which the client has no control. There were a variety of reactions. A few people decided to leave me before I left them. Some ended therapy sooner than they should have; others really got down to work and accomplished in two months more than in the previous two years.

My departure brought up issues of loss through death, particularly loss of mother or mother figures. Some clients had anger to work through; others reacted with tears. I told each one separately, of course, at a time in their session when it seemed appropriate to let them know. Some, especially women my age who were still working, wanted to know more about what the decision meant for me. Although it was my policy not to talk about myself, I felt I could briefly share a few facts about my own life, and then turn the spotlight back to their process. Although this shifted our relationship—I was not, in those moments, strictly in the role of therapist, but simply sharing as one woman to another—I sensed an implicit confirmation in lifting the imbalance between "therapist" and "client" to one of equality.

After all my current clients knew of my decision, I sent a letter to every client I had seen in the past two years who was not currently in treatment, as well as to long-term clients who had been in and out of therapy over many years. I wanted to let them know personally, before they one day phoned and got a message telling them my number had been disconnected. I also wanted them to have an opportunity to come back, if they wished, to say goodbye. Some had left with the intention of returning "one day"; now that option would soon be gone.

Over the course of the final year, when I took no one new, I had time to see many "returnees" who responded when they received my letter. These were sessions of affirmations and farewells, a bittersweet time. During the final month I sent another letter, this time to my current clients, thanking them for sharing their process with me and supplying them with names of other psychologists if they wanted to continue therapy in the future. I also told them how to get in touch with me after I closed my office. While very few did that, I wanted them to know that I was available; to realize that although I was closing my office, I was not dead and could still be reached. For most, that seemed to be reassuring.

I found a colleague to take over my space and the group signed a new lease without me. A young psychiatrist, just setting up a new office for her private practice, purchased most of my furniture. My office-mates invited our friends and colleagues to a farewell party. I packed my file cabinet, books and other sundries into my son's mini-van and moved them to my basement.

On a few occasions, I returned to be part of the Tuesday peer-group supervision meeting, but it was not the same. I loved the welcome I received and enjoyed sharing lunch and news of trips and grandchildren with my dear friends. But the discussion of cases no longer fascinated me. My life as a psychotherapist had come to a close.

Epilogue:
Remembering

Some time after I closed my office, while shopping at a local supermarket, I bumped into a former client in front of Campbell's soups. I recognized her immediately, although I had not seen her for five years. The computer in my brain brought up my imagined images of her children, her husband, her parents, her childhood, and several dreams she had told me about. I asked about her health, and remembered that she had just switched to a new job before leaving therapy. I remembered exactly in which room of which clinic we met when each of these people and events in her life was discussed.

I could recall everything about her except her name.

My fading memory for proper nouns had been a handicap that I tried to conceal, not always successfully. Once, after a particularly intense and fruitful session with a woman named Kate, I said, as she was going out the door, "Good-bye, I'll see you next week, Kathy." I knew who Kate was, and what her name was. I couldn't believe what had just come out of my mouth. Kathy was my next client. What would I call her, if I wasn't more careful? I felt I had blown the entire hour. If your psychotherapist can't remember your name, after you have just revealed some of the most painful moments of your life to her, was the therapy worth continuing?

Fortunately, Kate returned the next week, and we were able to talk about my error. It was not nearly as devastating for her as it had been for me.

I once had a colleague who never kept notes. One month there was going to be a Blue Cross audit, and she had to update her files, going back months. I could not imagine how she was going to accomplish this, without making it up. My notes were complete, not because I was a superior person, but because the only way I could remember the specific content of the session was to write the notes immediately after the client left, and before the next client came in. "How ever will you get those notes done?" I asked my friend. I was in shock at the very thought of it.

"It's not hard", she said. "I have a movie running in my head of everything that happened at every session, for each client. I just have to turn on the movie screen, and the writing is easy."

That fascinated me. Even when I go to the movies, the real movies, I have forgotten the details of the plot by the next day. I remember the general story, the theme, the philosophy and all the characters. But I forget the details, and often forget the ending. How could anyone possibly recall every detail of every therapy session, especially if there were thirty or more sessions a week, for as many as twelve weeks? If I had to put that much energy into writing something, I thought, I would chose to write a novel.

I once had a colleague who had a memory problem much more serious than mine. At least she had an excuse: she had been in a serious auto accident and suffered a closed head injury, which severely impaired her short-term memory. She was a brilliant woman and was able to be of help to her clients despite her handicap. Her doctor had suggested that she take notes during the session, so that her notes were complete by the time the client left the room. She did that, and found it helpful.

I did not like to write while someone was talking, unless it was the first session and I needed to keep track of a detailed history. I preferred to give my full attention to the speaker. I found that writing the notes immediately after the session was easy to do. The entire hour was fresh in my mind, with no other distractions. Often I included in my notes a suggestion to myself for the next session: "Ask about job interview," or "Ask about trip to NY last weekend." That way, I was in tune with my clients' current life happenings and they were impressed with my excellent memory.

During the session, I was completely focused on the content and process of the session, so that when the client said, "What was I just telling you?" I could remind her, "You just started to tell me about your son's teacher, when that fire engine screamed by." (A psychoanalyst would probably say, "What does it mean, that you don't remember what you were talking about?" thus adding another problem to an already troubled life. I was so grateful that I remembered that I never considered making an issue of it.)

I only wrote first names in my appointment book, sometimes with a last initial, if I had more than one client with the same first name. I did that in case I lost my book, so clients could not be identified by someone finding it. Occasionally, just before I began a session, I could not remember the last name. Again, I could remember every intimate detail of the person's last ten sexual encounters, but unless I had that last name, I could not converse undistracted. I learned to always look at the folder before the session.

Despite these lapses with names, I have never forgotten the people. All who crossed the threshold of my office remain indelibly outlined in my memory: how they looked, how they behaved in therapy, the nature of their difficulty in life, their dream imagery and their childhoods. All are stored in the computer files of my brain. Nameless, forever.

Glossary with Suggested Readings

Bioenergetics: A therapy that works directly with accessing emotion through freeing body structure. Read anything by its founder, Alexander Lowen.

Cognitive Therapy works primarily with logical thought and the uncovering of illogical or irrational belief systems that underlie such states as depression and anxiety.

Cognitive Therapy and the Behavioral Disorders, by Aaron T. Beck, MD

Ericksonian Hypnosis: The techniques used by Milton Erickson were different from those of standard hypnosis. He utilized the language and frame of reference of the client in his therapy, embedded suggestions in long teaching stories, and was said to be extremely effective in producing lasting change in one or two sessions.

Uncommon Therapy: the Psychiatric Techniques of Milton H. Erickson, MD, by Jay Haley

Family therapy: Several family therapists of major stature believed in bringing in as many family members as possible. Mental health professionals working with families may be interested in the following books:

The Family Crucible, by Napier and Whitaker

Satir Step by Step: A Guide to Creating change in Families, by Virginia Satir and Michele Baldwin

Family Therapy Techniques, by Salvador Minuchin

Techniques of Family Therapy, by Jay Haley

Gestalt Therapy: "Fritz" Perls, the originator of Gestalt therapy, was an outrageous character who worked out many creative techniques for therapy, usually done with one person at a time but in a group setting. His goal was to bring feelings from the past into the present moment. Rather than talking *about* your mother, he instructed you to see her in the empty chair facing you and talk *directly to* her. This powerful technique often brought up the important-but-buried feelings necessary to reach resolution. In the '70's and '80s, many group therapists effectively combined TA theory with Gestalt techniques.

The Gestalt Approach and Eyewitness to Therapy, by Frederick S. Perls;

Gestalt Therapy Integrated, by Irving Polster and Miriam Polster

Humanistic Psychology is a branch of theory and practice which holds that such intangibles as meaning, purpose and will are intrinsic to human nature and should be included in the process of treating the whole person. Some of its early founders/writers are names that became familiar to the general population: Carl Rogers, Abraham Maslow, Rollo May and Clark Moustakas among them.

Jungian dream work: Carl Gustav Jung was a Swiss psychiatrist who may have been many decades ahead of his time. He wrote about the collective unconscious and the power of symbols many years before most of the world was ready to understand.

Memories, Dreams, Reflections, or *Dreams;* also try *Dream Theaters of the Soul: Empowering the Feminine through Jungian Dream Work,* by Jean Benedict Raffa

Multiple Personality Disorder: This term is no longer officially used as a diagnostic category under Dissociative Disorders in the DSM IV. It is used here because that is what it was called in the '80's, when this chapter takes place, and that is how it is known by a majority of the public. Even though the name has been changed, the condition itself still exists; however, now it is called Dissociative Identity Disorder (DID).

DID usually develops in very early childhood as a creative defense against remembering traumatic events, such as physical or sexual abuse. The very young child develops more than one personality in order to function in the world. In the story here, Betty Jean divided her memories from a very young age: Jean appeared "normal" and Betty remained hidden, trapped in a terror-filled childhood. (Many other alters formed over the years, as well; this is purposely over-simplified.)

Not every child who is abused becomes dissociative, but it is quite certain that every client with DID experienced some sort of severe trauma at a very early age, when the personality was just developing. By adulthood, the client's personal history and memories have become so fragmented that she has no inner sense of being a whole, cohesive person.

Unfortunately, dissociation is not easy to recognize. It is not uncommon to find that a DID client has been to many psychotherapists over a span of years, one diagnosing and treating her for depression, another for schizophrenia, a third for borderline personality disorder and so forth. Without proper diagnosis, treatment usually fails to address the person's inner fragmentation, which is the basic source of her distress. To treat the whole person, the therapist must work toward bringing the various inner parts of the client into contact with one another until she can function in her life as a unified personality with a cohesive life history.

If you are a therapist and want to read more, an excellent basic book is *The Diagnosis and Treatment of Multiple Personality Disorder*, by Frank W. Putnam. (It was written before the name-change, but it is still valid.)

Psychotherapy is done by mental health professionals with one of several degrees: Psychiatry (MD); Psychology (MA, PhD or PsyD); Social Work (MSW) or an MA in Counseling. The therapist's title reflects academic training. How skillfully psychotherapy is carried out, however, has as much to do with the person doing it as with the formal degree they hold. Only MDs can prescribe psychotropic medications at the present time in the U.S.

Transactional Analysis is an evolving system of theory and practice that made psychology accessible to the masses by using simple language, diagrams and humor in pointing out, clearly, non-useful patterns of behavior. It was introduced by Eric Berne in a series of books in the 1970's and became popularized across the country as an accessible way to understand many principles of psychology which had been obscure to the general public. Such terms as "Parent-Adult-Child" ego states and "I'm OK, You're OK" life positions became part of common parlance. Training toward certification in TA was widely available to psychotherapists in North American and Western Europe. Eric Berne wrote a number of books, not all of which are still in print. You might want to read:

Games People Play, by Eric Berne, MD

TA Today: A New Introduction to Transactional Analysis, by Ian Stewart and Van Joines.

0-595-32494-0

.

Printed in the United States
40493LVS00018B/29

9 780595 324941